A GLOSSARY OF
CORPUS LINGUISTICS

D0862172

TITLES IN THE SERIES INCLUDE

A Glossary of
Corpus Linguistics

*Paul Baker, Andrew Hardie
and Tony McEnery*

Edinburgh University Press

© Paul Baker, Andrew Hardie and Tony McEnery, 2006

Edinburgh University Press Ltd
22 George Square, Edinburgh

Typeset in Sabon
by Norman Tilley Graphics, Northampton,
and printed and bound in Finland
by WS Bookwell

A CIP record for this book is
available from the British Library

ISBN-10 0 7486 2403 1 (hardback)
ISBN-13 978 0 7486 2403 4
ISBN-10 0 7486 2018 4 (paperback)
ISBN-13 978 0 7486 2018 0

The right of Paul Baker, Andrew Hardie and
Tony McEnery to be identified as authors of this
work has been asserted in accordance with the
Copyright, Designs and Patents Act 1988.

Published with the support of the Edinburgh
University Scholarly Publishing Initiatives Fund

Introductory Notes

Website Addresses

We have tried to avoid referring to website addresses where possible, as we found that some of the websites we included at the start of writing this book were no longer in existence when we reached the final stages. We have included websites of some organisations, groups, corpora or software where we feel that the site is unlikely to close down or move. However, we cannot vouch for the longevity of all of the websites given here. If readers wish to follow up specific terms on the internet and are taken to a dead link, we suggest that they accept our apologies and then try a reputable search engine like www.google.com (assuming that Google still exists!).

List of Acronyms

Corpus linguistics is a discipline that has yielded a prolific number of acronyms. This presents a problem in terms of consistency: some terms are best known by their acronym, others are best known by their full-name. We want to make the ordering of dictionary entries consistent, yet we also want them to be easy to find. So, in ordering dictionary entries we have made the decision to spell out all acronyms as full words, while including a list of all of the acronyms at the beginning of the dictionary along with their full titles. Therefore, readers who want to use this dictionary to find out about the **BNC** can look up its full title in the acronym list at the beginning of the book, and then go to the dictionary entry under **British National Corpus.**

ACASD (Automatic Content Analysis of Spoken Discourse) word sense tagging system
ACE (Australian Corpus of English)
ACH (Association for Computers and the Humanities)
ACL (Association for Computational Linguistics)
ACLDCI (Association for Computational Linguistics Data Collection Initiative)
AGTK (Annotation Graph Toolkit)
AHI (American Heritage Intermediate) Corpus
ALLC (Association for Literary and Linguistic Computing)
AMALGAM (Automatic Mapping Among Lexico-Grammatical Annotation Models) Tagger
ANC (American National Corpus)
ANLT (Alvey Natural Language Tools)
AP (Associated Press) Treebank
APHB (American Printing House for the Blind) Treebank
ARCHER (Representative Corpus of Historical English Registers) Corpus
ASCII (American Standard Code for Information Exchange)
ATC (Air Traffic Control) Corpus
AUTASYS (Automatic Text Annotation System) Tagger
BAS (Bavarian Archive for Speech Signals)
BASE (British Academic Spoken English) Corpus
BNC (British National Corpus)
BoE (Bank of English)
CALL (Computer Assisted Language Learning)
CAMET (Computer Archive of Modern English Texts)
CANCODE (Cambridge and Nottingham Corpus of Discourse in English)
CEEC (Corpus of Early English Correspondence)
CEG (Cronfa Electroneg o Gymraeg)
CELEX (Centre for Lexical Information)

CES (Corpus Encoding Standard)

CETH (Centre for Electronic Texts in the Humanities)

CHAT (Codes for the Human Analysis of Transcripts) System

CHILDES (Child Language Data Exchange System)

CIDE (Collaborative International Dictionary of English)

CLAN (Computerized Language Analysis) System

CLAWS (Constituent Likelihood Automatic Word-tagging System)

CLEC (Chinese Learner English Corpus)

CLR (Consortium for Lexical Research)

CMU SLM (Carnegie Mellon University–Cambridge Statistical Language Modeling) Toolkit

Coconut (Cooperative, Coordinated Natural Language Utterances) Corpus

COLT (Bergen Corpus of London Teenage English)

CRATER (Corpus Resources and Terminology Extraction)

CSAE (Corpus of Spoken American English)

CSLU (Centre for Spoken Language Understanding) Speech Corpora

CSTR (Centre for Speech Technology Research)

CWBC (Corpus of Written British Creole)

DAT (Dialogue Annotation Tool)

DCPSE (Diachronic Corpus of Present-day Spoken English)

DTD (document type definition)

EACL (European Chapter of the Association for Computational Linguistics)

EAGLES (Expert Advisory Group on Language Engineering Standards)

ECI (European Corpus Initiative)

ELAN (Eudico Linguistic Annotator)

ELAN (European Language Activity Network)

ELDA (Evaluations and Language Resources Distribution Agency)

ELRA (European Language Resources Association)

ELSNET (European Network of Excellence in Human Language Technologies)

EMILLE (Enabling Minority Language Engineering) Corpus

ENGCG (Constraint Grammar Parser of English)

ESFSLD (European Science Foundation Second Language Databank)

FLOB (Freiburg–LOB Corpus of British English)

FRIDA (French Interlanguage Database)

FROWN (Freiburg–Brown Corpus of American English)

FTF (Fuzzy Tree Fragments)

GATE (General Architecture for Text Engineering)

GPEC (Guangzhou Petroleum English Corpus)

HCRC (Human Communication Research Centre)

HKUST (Hong Kong University Of Science And Technology) Corpus

HLT (human language technology)

HTML (Hypertext Markup Language)

ICAME (International Computer Archive of Modern and Medieval English)

ICE (International Corpus of English)

ICECUP (International Corpus of English Corpus Utility Program)

ICLE (International Corpus of Learner English)

IMS (Institut für Maschinelle Sprachverarbeitung)

ISLE (Interactive Spoken Language Education) Corpus

IviE (Intonational Variation in English) Corpus

KWIC (key word in context)

LCMC (Lancaster Corpus of Mandarin Chinese)

LCPW (Lancaster Corpus of Children's Project Writing)

LDB (Linguistic DataBase)

LDC (Linguistic Data Consortium)

LeaP (Learning the Prosody of a Foreign Language) Corpus

Lindsei (Louvain International Database of Spoken English Interlanguage)

LLC (London–Lund Corpus)

LOB (Lancaster–Oslo/Bergen) Corpus
MARSEC (Machine-Readable Spoken English Corpus)
MBT (Memory Based Tagger)
METER (Measuring Text Reuse) Corpus
MICASE (Michigan Corpus of Academic Spoken English)
MTP (Münster Tagging Project)
MXPOST (Maximum Entropy Part-of-Speech Tagger)
NECTE (Newcastle Electronic Corpus of Tyneside English)
NEET (Network of Early Eighteenth Century English Texts)
NITCS (Northern Ireland Transcribed Corpus of Speech)
NLP (natural language processing)
OCP (Oxford Concordance Programme)
OCR (optical character recognition)
OLAC (Open Language Archives Community)
OTA (Oxford Text Archive)
POS (part-of-speech) tagging
POW (Polytechnic of Wales) corpus
SARA (SGML-Aware Retrieval Application)
ScoSE (Saarbrücken Corpus of Spoken English)
SEC (Lancaster/IBM Spoken English Corpus)
SEU (Survey of English Usage) Corpus
SGML (Standard Generalised Markup Language)
SPAAC (Speech Act Annotated Corpus for Dialogue Systems)
SUSANNE (Surface and Underlying Structural Analyses of Naturalistic English) Corpus
TEI (Text Encoding Initiative)
TELC (Thai English Learner Corpus)
TESS (Text Segmentation for Speech) Project
TLFi (Trésor de la Langue Française Informatisé)
TLG (Thesaurus Linguae Graecae)
TnT (Trigrams'n'Tags)
TOSCA (Tools for Syntactic Corpus Analysis) Corpus
T2K-SWAL (TOEFL 2000 Spoken and Written Academic Language Corpus)

UAM (Universidad Autónoma de Madrid) Spanish Treebank
UCREL (University Centre for Computer Corpus Research on Language)
USAS (UCREL Semantic Analysis System)
WBE (Wolverhampton Business English Corpus)
WSC (Wellington Corpus of Spoken New Zealand English)
WWC (Wellington Corpus of Written New Zealand English)
Xaira (XML Aware Indexing and Retrieval Architecture)
XML (Extensible Markup Language)
YCOE (York–Toronto–Helsinki Corpus of Old English Prose)
ZEN (Zürich English Newspaper Corpus)

accented characters In order to ensure that the text within a corpus can be rendered in the same way across different platforms it is recommended that some form of recognised encoding system for accented characters is employed. The **Text Encoding Initiative** (TEI) guidelines suggests encoding accented characters as entities, using the characters & and ; to mark the beginning and end of the entity respectively. Table 1 shows a few accented characters and their corresponding encodings. A couple of examples of entity references for fractions and currency are also shown below. (See also **punctuation marks.**)

accuracy A basic score for evaluating automatic **annotation tools** such as **parsers** or **part-of-speech taggers.** It is equal to the number of **tokens** correctly tagged, divided by the total number of tokens. This is usually expressed as a percentage. Typical accuracy rates for state-of-the-art English part-of-speech taggers are in range of 95 per cent to 97 per cent. (See also **precision and recall.**)

Acquilex Projects The two Acquilex projects were funded by the European Commission and were based at Cambridge University. The first project explored the utility of constructing a multilingual lexical knowledge base from machine-readable versions of conventional **dictionaries.**

Table 1. Sample of entity references for accented characters, fractions and currency

encoding	character description	character
&auml;	Small letter a with umlaut (or diaersis)	ä
&aacute;	Small letter a with acute accent	á
&egrave;	Small letter e with grave	è
&ocirc;	Small letter o with circumflex accent	ô
&atilde;	Small letter a with tilde	ã
&aelig;	Small ligature ae	æ
&frac14;	Fraction symbol: one quarter.	¼
&pound;	Pound symbol	£

The second project explored the utility of machine-readable textual **corpora** as a source of lexical information not coded in conventional dictionaries, and looked at adding dictionary publishing partners to exploit the lexical **database** and corpus extraction software developed by the projects for conventional lexicography. See http://www.cl.cam.ac.uk/Research/NL/acquilex/acqhome.html.

Air Traffic Control (ATC) Corpus A corpus composed of recordings of conversations between air traffic controllers and airline pilots from Dallas Fort Worth, Logan International and Washington National airports. The corpus contains approximately seventy hours of such material. The original sound recordings are available and each conversation has been orthographically transcribed. The corpus is available from the **Linguistic Data Consortium.**

Alex Catalogue of Electronic Texts An **archive** of on-line, freely available texts that are copyright free. The catalogue holds classics of British and American literature as well as some titles relating to Western philosophy. Alex has a rudimentary author/title search interface to assist users in finding texts to download. Alex currently contains approximately 600 texts.

alignment When working on a **parallel corpus,** it is useful to know exactly which parts of a text in language A correspond to the equivalent corresponding text in language B. The process of adding such information to parallel texts is called alignment. Alignment can be carried out at the *sentence level*, in which case each sentence is linked to the sentence it corresponds to in the other language(s). This is not straightforward, as the sentence breaks are not necessarily in the same place in a translation as they are in the original text.

Alternatively, alignment can be done at the *word level*, in which case each word must be linked to a word or words in the parallel text. This is much more complex, as a given word may correspond to one word, more than one word, or no word at all in the other language, and the word order may be different as well. For example, English *I saw it* would correspond to French *je l'ai vu*, where *I = je, saw = ai vu*, and *it = l'*. However, word alignment is also much more useful than sentence alignment, for example, for finding translation equivalents and compiling bilingual **lexicons**.

When a **spoken corpus** is released alongside the sound recordings from which it was created, the text may contain **markup** to show the point in time in the recording to which each chunk of text corresponds. This is also referred to as alignment (more specifically, *time-alignment* or *temporal alignment*). (See also **machine translation**.)

Alvey Natural Language Tools (ANLT) A set of tools for use in natural language processing research, created at the Universities of Cambridge, Edinburgh and Lancaster between the late 1980s and early 1990s. These include a morphological analyser, a grammar, two parsers and a lexicon containing 63,000 entries. They can be used independently or with a grammar development environment to form a complete system for the morphological, syntactic and semantic analysis of English. The tools are run on a Unix platform.

ambiguity In corpus **annotation,** in cases where there is a choice of two potential tags at one point in the text, it is not always possible to make a clear-cut decision. For example, in **part-of-speech tagging,** it is sometimes difficult to determine the grammatical categories of certain words as, for instance, in the following:

> I *put* it down. (Is *put* the past participle or past tense form?)
> Bill was *married*. (Is *married* an adjective or verb?)
> It*'s* broken. (Is *'s* a contraction of *has* or *is*?)
> There is a question on *gardening*. (Is gardening a noun or verb?)

In some cases a **portmanteau tag** can be given in order to address the ambiguity. In others, examining more of the surrounding context may help to solve the problem. However, in extremely ambiguous cases, the corpus builder may have to make a decision one way or the other. If this approach is taken then the decision would need at least to be applied with **consistency** throughout the corpus. In general, decisions regarding ambiguous cases should be covered in the **documentation** that comes with a corpus.

American Heritage Intermediate (AHI) Corpus A commercial corpus of 5.09 million words based on a survey in 1969 of American schools, consisting of 10,043 samples of texts that were widely read among American children aged between seven and fifteen years. It was originally produced in order to provide a citation base for the *American Heritage School Dictionary*.

American National Corpus (ANC) A **part-of-speech tagged** corpus of American English, containing both written and spoken data, produced from 1990 onwards. Work on the corpus began in 1998 and is still in progress at the time of writing. It will contain a core of 100 million words, making it comparable to the **British National Corpus (BNC)**. The **genres** in the ANC include newer types of language data that have become available since the latter part of the twentieth century, such as web-based diaries (blogs), web pages, chats, email, and rap music lyrics. Beyond this, it will include an additional component of several hundred million words. It is encoded in **XML**. See Reppen and Ide (2004).

American Printing House for the Blind (APHB) Treebank The APHB corpus was developed in a collaboration between Lancaster University (UK) and IBM T. J. Watson Research Center (USA). The corpus is composed of a number of works of fiction that had been converted to machine readable form by the APHB. The data was **part-of-speech tagged** using the CLAWS part-of-speech tagger. The output from CLAWS was corrected by hand. The corpus was then manually parsed using a **skeleton parsing** scheme (Eyes and Leech, 1993). Some 200,000 words were parsed to form the so-called APHB Treebank. The corpus has never been released into the public domain.

American Standard Code for Information Exchange (ASCII)
A **character set** based on the Roman writing script used in modern English and other Western European languages. It is a seven-bit code, meaning that each character is stored as seven binary digits. A binary digit can only be 0 or 1, meaning that only 128 characters can be encoded in ASCII. The first thirty-two codes (numbers 0–31 decimal) in ASCII are used as control characters (codes that control devices such as printers). Code 32 is a space character, while codes 33 to 126 are printable characters, consisting of the following letters, numbers, symbols and punctuation:

!"#$%&'()*+,./0123456789:;<=>?@ABCDEFGHIJK LMNOPQRSTUVWXYZ[\]^_`abcdefghijklmnopqrst uvwxyz{|}~

The final code, 127, is a delete or rub-out character. ASCII is only suitable for encoding text that occurs in romanised scripts. An extended form of ASCII uses 8-bit character encodings, or 256 charcters. This allows characters used in East European or Cyrillic languages to be encoded in the top half of the system. (See also **Unicode**.)

Anaphoric Treebank Developed in a collaboration between Lancaster University (UK) and IBM T. J. Watson Research Center (USA), the **corpus** was based upon newswire stories from the **Associated Press** (AP) news agency. The AP texts were **part-of-speech tagged** and manually parsed using a **skeleton parsing** scheme. Approximately 1 million words of AP newswire material was tagged and parsed in this manner. From this data, 100,000 words of the Treebank were annotated to show co-reference relationships in the text, using a scheme devised by Fligelstone (1992). The corpus has never been released into the public domain.

annotation The process of applying additional information to corpus data. See **encoding, tagging**.

Annotation Graph Toolkit (AGTK) A suite of software which supports the application of annotation graphs to audio and video data. Using AGTK one can readily develop a tool which can aid in the process of the **annotation** of such data. See http://agtk.sourceforge.net/.

anonymisation As a point of **ethics,** corpus texts need to be made anonymous where necessary by removing personal names and other identifying details (or substituting them with codes, pseudonyms etc.). While there is no need to make published texts or transcriptions of radio or TV broadcasts anonymous, as their content is not confidential, unpublished writings or transcriptions of personal conversations should have the names removed so that the writers or speakers cannot be identified. Examples of **corpora** with anonymisation are the **Cambridge Learner Corpus** (written) or the spoken section of the **BNC**.

AntConc A freeware **concordancer** developed by Laurence Anthony which runs on the Linux operating system. AntConc offers a variety of basic corpus query tools including **keyword** extraction, KWIC concordancing and **word list** generation. See http://www.antlab.sci. waseda.ac.jp/.

Apple Pie Parser An automated **parser** developed as part of the Proteus project at New York University by Satoshi Sekine and Ralph Grishman (Sekine and Grishman, 1995). This is a probabilistic parser which was initially trained on the **Penn Treebank**. The analyses produced by the parser follow the Penn Treebank parsing scheme prior to version II of the Penn Treebank. The system is available to run both on **Unix** and Windows machines. The system has a reported **accuracy** rate of 77.18 per cent at time of writing. It is available from http://nlp. cs.nyu.edu/app/.

applications of corpus linguistics Hunston (2002: 1) writes 'It is no exaggeration to say that **corpora,** and the study of corpora, have revolutionised the study of language, and of the applications of language, over the last few decades.' Since the 1980s corpus linguistics has been applied, among other ways, to dictionary creation (Clear et al. 1996), as an aid to interpretation of literary texts (Louw 1997), in forensic linguistics (Woolls and Coulthard 1998), language description (Sinclair 1999), in language **variation** studies (Biber 1988) and in the production of **language teaching** materials (Johns 1997). Corpus data has also informed studies of first and second language acquisition (see, for example, MacWhinney 1991, Granger 1998, Granger et al. 2002a). Other studies have shown how corpus analysis can uncover discourses and evidence for disadvantage (see Hunston 2002: 109–23 for a summary). **Multilingual corpora** are also useful in translation studies (e.g. Baker 1993). Finally, in psycholinguistics Garnham et al.'s (1981) study used the **London–Lund Corpus** to examine the occurrence of speech errors in natural conversational English.

approximate string matching In **information retrieval** when a **string** is being searched for in a collection of data that may contain errors. Given the case of a search for spelling errors, for example, we would like to find strings that are *almost* the same as the search string, as well as strings that are *exactly* the same as the search string. For example, if we were searching for *government* but we would like to pick up spelling mistakes for *government* too (for example, *governmant*), this could be accomplished using approximate string matching.

archive Generally defined as being similar to a **corpus**, although with some significant differences. Geoffrey Leech (1991: 11) suggests that 'the difference between an archive and a corpus must be that the latter is designed for a particular "representative" function'. An archive, on the other hand, is simply 'a text repository, often huge and opportunistically collected, and normally not structured' (Kennedy 1998: 4).

Asian Newspaper English An on-line concordance derived from a corpus of 114,502 words gathered from newspapers published in English in eighteen Asian countries. The system, developed at the University of Hong Kong, is no longer on-line.

Associated Press Treebank A **skeleton-parsed** 1-million-word corpus of American newswire reports. (See also **treebank**.)

Association for Computers and the Humanities (ACH) Along with the **Association for Literary and Linguistic Computing (ALLC)**, the ACH is one of the two major international professional organisations in corpus-based studies of language and literature. Formed in the 1960s, the ACH publishes a journal, *Computers in the Humanities* and is concerned with the development and analysis of text databases as well as research in the humanities and social sciences. See www.ach.org.

Association for Computational Linguistics (ACL) An international scientific and professional society for people carrying out research on natural language and computation. The ACL publishes a quarterly journal *Computational Linguistics* and organises conferences. See www.aclweb.org.

Association for Computational Linguistics Data Collection Initiative (ACLDCI) The ACLDCI makes a number of texts available in **Text Encoding Initiative (TEI)**-conformant markup. These texts mainly consist of American English, including a selection of the *Wall Street Journal*, material from the **Penn Treebank** Project, the *Collins English Dictionary* (1979 edition) and transcripts of Canadian parliamentary proceedings (Hansard) in French and English aligned format. See Church and Liberman (1991).

Association for Literary and Linguistic Computing (ALLC) The ALLC is concerned with the application of computing in the study of language and literature. Formed in 1973, the ALLC's membership is international, comprising students and researchers from across the humanities disciplines. The ALLC's journal, *Literary and Linguistic Computing*, is published by Oxford University Press. It holds a joint annual conference with the **Association for Computers and the Humanities (ACH)**, usually alternating between North America and Europe. See www. kcl.ac.uk/humanities/cch/allc/.

attested data Also *actual* or *authentic data*. This term denotes data that occur naturally and have been transcribed or recorded accordingly, without intervention from the researcher (Stubbs 2001: xiv). (See also **modified data** and **intuitive data**.)

Augustan Prose Sample An example of **historical corpus** data. The Augustan Prose Sample consists of extracts of writing by many English authors during the period 1678 to 1725. Milić (1990) gives details of the rationale behind this corpus and its later development. (See also the **Century of Prose Corpus.**)

Australian Corpus of English (ACE) The first systematically compiled heterogeneous corpus in Australia, consisting of 1 million words of Australian English based on 500 samples of text each consisting of 2,000 words. The ACE matches the **Brown** and **Lancaster–Oslo/Bergen (LOB) corpora** in most aspects of its structure, although it contains material from 1986. It was compiled at the department of Linguistics at Macquarie University NSW Australia. See Collins and Peters (1988).

authorship identification The field of text analysis which attempts to ascertain whether a given text was written by a particular author or not, usually by automatic and/or statistical methods. The use of a corpus is often essential to authorship identification as the text must be compared to a large number of other texts by the suspected author(s), and also a large number of texts *not* by the suspected author, to establish whether the statistical patterns found in the text are more like the former than the latter.

Automatic Content Analysis of Spoken Discourse (ACASD) word sense tagging system A form of semantic annotation which works on text that has been **part-of-speech tagged** using the **CLAWS** tagging system. See Wilson and Rayson (1993). (See also **UCREL semantic analysis system (USAS).**)

Automatic Mapping Among Lexico-Grammatical Annotation Models (AMALGAM) Tagger A project undertaken by a team led by Eric Atwell at the University of Leeds (UK) which sought to map correspondences between different **part-of-speech** tagsets and **parsing** schemes. As part of the project, a **tagger** was developed which could **annotate** a text with any one of up to eight different part-of-speech tagsets. The tagger is available via email, and there are plans to make this tagging service available via the web. See http://www.comp.leeds. ac.uk/amalgam/amalgam/amalghome.htm.

Automatic Text Annotation System (AUTASYS) Tagger A menu-driven MS-DOS based **part-of-speech tagger** for English developed by Alex Chengyu Fang (see Fang, 1996). It can tag words with one of three part-of-speech **tagsets** (the LOB, ICE and SKELETON tagsets). The system is generally available though users must pay a licence fee for the software. See http://www.phon.ucl.ac. uk/home/alex/project/tagging/tagging.htm.

B

balanced corpus A corpus that contains texts from a wide range of different language **genres** and text domains, so that, for example, it may include both spoken and written, and public and private texts. Balanced **corpora** are sometimes referred to as **reference**, *general* or *core* corpora.

Bank of English (BoE) The BoE is both a **reference corpus** and **monitor corpus** of general English launched in 1991 by COBUILD (a division of HarperCollins publishers) and The University of Birmingham. The BoE consisted of 525 million words of spoken and written language in

April 2005. The majority of texts reflect British English but some are from North American sources and other native varieties of English. See Jarvinen (1994).

Baum–Welch algorithm (or *Forward–Backwards algorithm*) A technique for training a **part-of-speech tagger** based on **probabilistic disambiguation** on untagged data. Normally, the **tag transition probabilities** used in a **hidden Markov model** are calculated by looking at the **frequency** of each pair of tags in a tagged corpus. However, it is possible to take some initial estimates of the transition probabilities (which need not be very good) and use the Baum–Welch algorithm to apply these estimates to a corpus of untagged data, and thus compute *improved* estimates. The **Xerox tagger** can be trained in this way.

Bavarian Archive for Speech Signals (BAS) Hosted at the University of Munich, Germany, this **archive** seeks to make spoken German resources accessible to all. Some of the holdings in the archive are available for commercial as well as academic use. The archive is extensive and varied and includes **corpora**, speech databases, reports and software. While largely of interest to speech scientists, some of the material held in the archive is almost certainly of interest to the general linguist or scholar of German. For example, the Hempel's Sofa Corpus contains a series of recorded spontaneous monologues produced in response to the question 'What did you do within the last hour?' See http://www.phonetik.uni-muenchen.de/Bas/BasHomeeng.html.

Bellcore The shortened name of the Bell Communications Research Corpus, collected in the USA, consisting of an **archive** of about 200 million words of newspaper wire text and 50 million words of other journalistic writing along with other bodies of texts such as the **Brown Corpus** and some English dictionaries.

Bergen Corpus of London Teenage English (COLT) A corpus of spontaneous speech gathered from London teenagers in the age range 13–17. The data was gathered in 1993. The project was led by Anna-Brita Stenström of the University of Bergen. Some of the COLT data appeared as part of the spoken section of the **British National Corpus (BNC)**. The COLT corpus is notable, however, for having the original sound recordings as well as **part-of-speech tagged** orthographic transcriptions of the conversations available. The corpus is around 500,000 words in size. See http://torvald.aksis. uib.no/colt/ or Stenström et al. (2002) for further details.

bigram and trigram The two most common types of **tag transition probabilities** used in a probabilistic **part-of-speech tagger**. A bigram probability is the probability of a sequence of *two* tags: that is, the probability that tag B will occur, given that it comes directly after tag A. A trigram probability is the probability of a sequence of *three* tags: that is, the probability that tag C will occur, given that it comes directly after a sequence of tag A followed by tag B. The main difference between bigram and trigram taggers is the amount of tagging data required to train them: trigram taggers require a lot more because, for any given **tagset**, there are many more possible three-tag sequences than possible two-tag sequences. There is some debate as to whether trigram taggers work better than bigram taggers. In theory they should, as they take more context into account. It has been suggested, however, that, in practice, any improvement they offer is tiny compared to the extra effort required to train them.

More generally, the different types of transition probabilities can be referred to as *N*-grams (and the type of tagger that uses them can be called an *N*-gram tagger). Although other values of N are possible in theory, in practice N is nearly always 2 or 3.

Birmingham Corpus A synonym for the **Bank of English (BoE)**.

Birmingham Email Tagging Service This **part-of-speech tagging** service is no longer available but is worthy of mention as it was the first email-based tagger to be made generally available. The system accepted text by email which was then part-of-speech tagged and returned to the sender. The system was developed by Oliver Mason and was based upon his Qtag system. For more information on the Qtag system, including a **Java**-based version of the program, which is freely available to download and use for academic research, see http://www.english.bham.ac.uk/staff/omason/software/qtag.html.

BNCweb A web-based tool used for searching and retrieving lexical, grammatical and textual data from the **British National Corpus (BNC)**. BNCweb was developed at the University of Zürich and enables users to carry out searches, view, sort and **thin concordances**, calculate **collocations** using a range of statistical measures, specify **tag**-based searches, carry out **distribution** analyses and create sub-**corpora**. It can be used with any web-browser via the internet. See http://escorp.unizh.ch/.

BNC Web Indexer A web-based interface which allows one to explore the BNC using an alternative, genre-based categorisation of the BNC files provided by David Lee. The index covers twenty-four spoken and forty-six written genres. The web-based index is freely available via http://www.comp.lancs.ac.uk/computing/research/ucrel/bncindex/, though users must go through a registration process before accessing the index.

body The body of a corpus text is the part that follows the **header**. While the header contains information about the text (**metadata**), the body contains the text itself (the actual data) plus any **markup** the text has been given.

boilerplate A fixed block of text which can be used without alteration in many documents. Boilerplate is an important issue in corpus building that takes text from the **World Wide Web**, because most web sites add boilerplate text around the actual document a page contains, for instance a menu bar, advertisement, list of links, or copyright notice. To avoid **duplicating** this text in each corpus file, it is necessary to remove the boilerplate. However, the massive variations found in **HTML** across the Web mean that this can be difficult to do automatically, while removing it manually, on the other hand, is impractical for very large **corpora**.

bootstrapping Derived from the expression 'to pull oneself up by one's bootstraps', this word describes a process often used in the development of corpus annotation **tools**, for example **taggers**. A tool is built quickly, with many weaknesses, and is used to analyse a corpus (perhaps with many mistakes). That corpus data is then used to improve the tool, perhaps by using it as training data. The improved tool is then used to analyse the corpus data again, this time with fewer errors. The sequence then repeats. Bootstrapping techniques allow good corpus annotation tools to be developed without having to manually annotate a large training corpus in advance.

Bow (aka libbow) A library of text processing procedures written in the **C programming language** designed to assist with statistical textual analysis. Bow was developed by a team led by Andrew McCallum at Carnegie Mellon University, USA. Bow has three subsets of procedures – rainbow, arrow and crossbow. Rainbow focuses on document classification, arrow covers document retrieval while crossbow covers document **clustering**. Bow is available for both academic and commercial research purposes. For more information see http://www-2.cs.cmu.edu/~mccallum/bow/.

Brill tagger A trainable, rule-based **part-of-speech tagger** (named after its creator, Eric Brill) that was originally developed for the English language. The tagger was written in the LISP programming language and was initially trained on the **Brown Corpus**. The fact that the Brill tagger was made freely available to other researchers and was retrainable meant that the program has become widely used and has been retrained to cover a range of languages. The tagger is available for download from http://www.cs.jhu.edu/~brill/. (See also Brill (1992).)

British Academic Spoken English (BASE) Corpus Under development at the Universities of Warwick and Reading in the UK, the BASE corpus has been developed to complement the **MICASE (Michigan Corpus of Academic Spoken English)** corpus from the USA. It is **Text Encoding Initiative (TEI)** conformant and is composed largely of video recordings of lectures and seminars which are available both as sound files and transcriptions. The corpus is structured within a sample frame covering four broad academic domains: Arts and Humanities, Social Studies and Sciences, Physical Sciences and Life and Medical Sciences. For details of the corpus see http://www.rdg.ac.uk/AcaDepts/ll/base_corpus/.

British National Corpus (**BNC**) An approximately 100-million-word **corpus** of written (90 per cent) and spoken (10 per cent) British English. The 4,124 texts mainly originate from the late 1980s and 1990s, although about 5.5 million words were first published between 1960 and 1984. The written texts consist of extracts from regional and national newspapers, specialist periodicals and journals for all ages and interests, academic books and popular fiction, published and unpublished letters and memoranda, school and university essays. The spoken part includes a large amount of unscripted informal conversation recorded by volunteers selected from different age, regional and social classes, together with language collected in different contexts ranging from formal business or government meetings to radio shows and phone-ins.

The corpus is **part-of-speech tagged** using the **CLAWS** C5 **tagset**. The project was carried out by a consortium led by Oxford University Press and includes academic research centres at Oxford and Lancaster University as well as the publishers Addison-Wesley Longman and Larousse Kingfisher Chambers. (See also **BNCweb**.)

British National Corpus sampler A subcorpus of the **British National Corpus** (**BNC**) consisting of about 2 million words or one-fiftieth of the whole corpus. The sampler corpus has been **part-of-speech tagged** using a more complex **tagset** than the rest of the corpus (the C7 tagset which has 135 tags as opposed to the C5 tagset which has 61 tags). In addition the tagging of the sampler has been manually checked and hand corrected, so its **accuracy** is very close to 100 per cent. The sampler consists of 50 per cent written and 50 per cent spoken texts and maintains a wide and balanced sample of texts from across the BNC.

Brooklyn–Geneva–Amsterdam Parsed Corpus of Old English (aka the Brooklyn Corpus) A selection of texts from the **Helsinki Corpus of English texts** which have been parsed. Each Helsinki sample is from 5,000 to 10,000 words in length and the corpus consists of 106,210 words of annotated text. In addition to parsed data, the corpus also includes glosses to modern English and morphological tagging. The corpus is the result of an Anglo/Dutch/Swiss/US collaboration. While still available, the corpus has been superseded by the **York–Toronto–Helsinki Corpus of Old English Prose (YCOE)**. See http://www-users.york.ac.uk/~sp20/corpus.html.

Brown Corpus A **corpus** of approximately 1 million words of written American English dating from 1961. It contains 500 samples of text, each of about 2,000 words. There are fifteen different **genre** categories: press reportage, press editorial, press reviews, religion, skills and hobbies, popular lore, belles lettres, miscellaneous, learned, general fiction, mystery and detective fiction, science fiction, adventure and western fiction, romance and love story and humour. It was created by Nelson Francis and Henry Kučera in the early 1960s and was one of the first machine-readable **corpora** ever built. Although it was undertaken during a climate of indifference and hostility towards corpus-based linguistic analysis, Francis and Kučera's work proved to be 'the standard in setting the pattern for the preparation and presentation of further bodies of data in English or other languages' as they hoped (1964: 2), inspiring the creation of other corpora. It is part of the **International Computer Archive of Modern and Medieval English (ICAME)** collection of corpora. (See also **Lancaster–Oslo/Bergen (LOB)**, **Freiburg–LOB Corpus of British English (FLOB)** and the **Freiburg–Brown Corpus of American English (FROWN)**.)

BulTreebank A **corpus** of Bulgarian parsed using a Head-Driven Phrase Structure Grammar (HPSG, see Gazdar et al., 1985) parsing scheme. The corpus is under development by a team including researchers from the Bulgarian Academy of Sciences. Kiril Simov is the leader of the project. In addition to parsing the corpus, the corpus is also being **part-of-speech tagged**. At the time of writing, 72 million words of Bulgarian has been collected for the project and the application of annotation to the data is an on-going task. For more details of the project see Simov et al. (2004a). To access resources produced by the BulTreebank project visit: http://www.bultreebank. org/.

Business Letters Corpus A **corpus** of business letters written by **L2** American English speakers with a Japanese **L1** background. The corpus was gathered by Yasumasa Someya of Aoyama Gakuin University, Japan. The corpus can be used via a web-based concordancer available at http://ysomeya.hp.infoseek.co.jp/. Via this interface a number of other **corpora** can be accessed, notably Someya's **Personal Letters Corpus**. The corpus consists of 209,461 words contained in 1,464 letters.

| C |

C programming language This programming language has frequently been used to create powerful corpus **annotation** software and other applications in **computational linguistics,** particularly programs designed for a **Unix** environment. For example, many **part-of-speech taggers** have been written in C.

Cambridge and Nottingham Corpus of Discourse in English (CANCODE) A 5-million-word spontaneous **spoken corpus** of English collected by Cambridge University Press and the University of Nottingham between 1995 and 2000. The corpus includes casual conversations, discussion, people working together, shopping and finding out information. The recordings have been coded according to the relationship between the speakers: whether they are intimates (living together), casual acquaintances, colleagues at work, or strangers.

Cambridge–Cornell Corpus of Spoken North American English A 22-million-word **spoken corpus** of North American English collected jointly by Cambridge University Press and Cornell University in the United States.

Cambridge International Corpus A 700-million-word **corpus** of written and spoken English that includes the **Cambridge and Nottingham Corpus of Discourse in English (CANCODE)** the **Cambridge–Cornell Corpus of Spoken North American English** and the **Cambridge Learner Corpus.**

Cambridge Learner Corpus A 20-million-word (at the time of writing) **corpus** of English writing from learners of

English built by Cambridge University Press and Cambridge ESOL. The texts are taken from anonymised exam scripts from 50,000 students in over 150 countries. See **learner corpus**.

Canadian Hansard Treebank A **skeleton-parsed corpus** of proceedings in the Canadian Parliament consisting of 750,000 words.

Carnegie Mellon University–Cambridge Statistical Language Modeling (CMU SLM) Toolkit **Unix**-based software and tools designed to help researchers undertaking automated language processing. The tools are extensive and useful, and include packages that can generate **word lists** as well as **bigram and trigram** frequencies from corpus data. The toolkit is available for download, free of charge, from http://svr-www.eng.cam.ac.uk/~prc14/toolkit.html. (See also Clarkson and Rosenfeld (1997).)

CECIL A software package designed to assist in the analysis of speech data. The software was mainly of use for tone and stress analysis. The PC version of the program required specialist hardware to run. The software has been succeeded by the **Speech Analysis Tools** software package among others.

Centre for Lexical Information (CELEX) Relational Database A **database** of lexical data created in the 1990s developed by CELEX at the Max Planck Institute for Psycholinguistics. It contains data on the vocabulary of Dutch, English and German. Apart from orthographic features, the database comprises representations of the phonological, morphological, syntactic and **frequency** properties of **lemmata**.

Center for Electronic Texts in the Humanities (CETH) A centre established in 1991 by Princeton and Rutgers Universities in the United States as a North American focus for the acquisition and dissemination of electronic text files in the humanities. See http://www.ceth.rutgers. edu/.

Centre for Speech Technology Research (CSTR) A research unit specialising in speech science research at the University of Edinburgh, UK. CSTR produced the Eustace **corpus**. This **speech corpus** is mainly of interest to speech scientists, being composed of a pre-selected set of sentences spoken aloud by six speakers of English. The corpus contains 4,608 sentences. See http://www. cstr.ed.ac.uk/ for further details.

Center for Spoken Language Understanding (CSLU) Speech Corpora A range of **speech corpora** developed at the Center for Spoken Language Understanding, Oregon University of Health and Science, USA. The **corpora** cover a range of languages including Eastern Arabic, Cantonese, Czech, Farsi, French, German, Hindi, Hungarian, Japanese, Korean, Malay, Mandarin, Italian, Polish, Portuguese, Russian, Spanish, Swedish, Swahili, Tamil, Vietnamese and English. The corpora are largely of interest to speech scientists, as they typically are not of spontaneous conversations, being composed of material elicited with speech applications in mind (for example, people repeating a list of commands). Some of the corpora are available with a range of annotations. Access to the corpora is gained either by joining the Center or by licensing individual corpora from CSLU. See http://cslu.cse.ogi.edu/corpora/corpCurrent.html.

Century of Prose Corpus A **diachronic corpus** of literary and non-literary English sampled from 120 authors between 1680 and 1780, including Burke, Swift and Gibbon. The corpus includes ten text categories and was compiled by Louis T. Milić. See Milić (1990) for more information. (See also the **Augustan Prose Sample**.)

Chadwyck-Healey Databases A number of **databases** of historical texts including *The Chadwyck-Healey English Poetry Full Text Database*, which contains most of the canon of English poetry from the Anglo-Saxon period to 1900 and contains over 4,500 volumes of poetry from 1,257 poets. *The Chadwyck-Healey English Verse Drama Full-Text Database* includes over 1,500 verse dramas by over 650 authors from the late thirteenth century to the late nineteenth century. Also included are *The African–American Poetry Full-Text Database 1760–1900* and *The American Poetry Full-Text Database*.

character set A term used to describe the digital representation of text. This usually involves identifying a collection of characters and assigning a number or value to each of them. Connolly (1995) defines a coded character set as 'A function whose domain is a subset of the integers, and whose range is a set of characters', noting that discussion of character representation is complex and often subtly inconsistent. A distinction should be made between characters and glyphs: a glyph is the visual rendering of a character (which is a somewhat abstract concept). We could define fonts as being sets of glyphs. For example, a character could be identified as 'Latin capital letter A' but could be represented by a variety of glyphs: A, A, **A** or *A*.

Historically the **American Standard Code for Information Exchange (ASCII)** character set has been used to represent modern English and other European languages. However, the **Unicode Standard** is a much larger character set that claims to cover writing systems for all of the world's languages.

ChaSen A **morphological analyser** for the Japanese language developed by the Computational Linguistics Laboratory, Graduate School of Information Science, Nara Institute of Science and Technology (NAIST). The system is available for downloading from: http://chasen.aist-nara.ac.jp/hiki/ChaSen/. The program runs on the Windows and Linux operating systems.

chi square A test for determining the significance of any numeric difference observed in data. The chi-squared test compares the difference between the observed values (e.g. the actual frequencies extracted from **corpora**) and the expected values (e.g. the frequencies that one would expect if no factor other than chance was affecting the frequencies). The greater the difference between the observed values and the expected values, the less likely it is that any difference is due to chance. Conversely, the closer the observed values are to the expected values, the more likely it is that the difference has arisen by chance. The chi-squared statistic is widely used, but is known to be unreliable when used with very low frequencies (frequencies less than 5, typically). Under such circumstances researchers have used the **log-likelihood** test. However even this statistic can be unreliable where low frequencies are concerned, so many researchers now use **Fisher's Exact Test** under these circumstances instead. See Oakes (1998) for more details of chi squared.

Child Language Data Exchange System (CHILDES) CHILDES is a system that provides tools for studying conversations, particularly those involving language acquisition. The system includes a **database** of transcript data from children and adults who are learning first and second languages, tools and guidelines for **encoding** and systems for linking transcripts to digitised audio and video. The data is transcribed in the **Codes for the Human Analysis of Transcripts (CHAT) System**. See http://childes.psy.cmu.edu/.

Chinese Learner English Corpus (CLEC) A corpus of **L2** English produced by **L1** Chinese speakers divided into five groups according to L2 English proficiency. The corpus was built by a team headed by Professor Gui Shichun at the Guangdong University of Foreign Studies, China. The corpus is approximately 1 million words in size and has been error tagged according to a scheme which classifies learner errors into sixty-one types. Both the corpus (on CD-ROM) and a description of the corpus (in Chinese) are available from the Shanghai Foreign Language Education Press. Email sflep@sflep. com.cn for details.

CHRISTINE Corpus Based upon a parsing scheme developed from the **SUSANNE** project and using **data** drawn from the spoken section of the **BNC**, the CHRISTINE corpus is a **treebank** of contemporary spoken British English. Comprehensive on-line documentation for the corpus is available at http://www.grsampson.net/ChrisDoc.html. The corpus can be downloaded, free of charge, for academic research from http://www. grsampson.net/Resources.html.

CLaRK An **Extensible Markup Language (XML)**-based system for **corpora** development created in a collaboration between the Seminar für Sprachwissenschaft,

Tübingen, Germany, and the Linguistic Modelling Laboratory, Bulgaria. The system is **Unicode** compliant and supports the manipulation and annotation of documents in the XML format. The system can be downloaded, free of charge, from http://www.bultreebank. org/clark/. More details of the system can be found in Simov et al. (2004b).

clitic A morpheme that has the syntactic characteristics of a word, but is phonologically and lexically bound to another word, for example *n't* in the word *hasn't*. Possessive forms can also be clitics, e.g. The dog*'s* dinner. When **part-of-speech tagging** is carried out on a corpus, clitics are often separated from the word they are joined to.

closure A term indicating that a particular feature in a variety of language is becoming finite. The more a **corpus** approaches closure, the more it approaches being completely representative of a language (or language variety). So, the more **representative** a corpus becomes, the lower the likelihood that new words, phrases or grammatical rules will be found. Lexical closure is defined as the point in a corpus beyond which the number of new lexical forms seen in every additional 1,000 tokens begins to level off at a rate lower than 10 per cent. See McEnery and Wilson (1996: 146–67) for studies of different types of closure in three **corpora**. Kovarik (2000), in his work on Chinese newspaper corpora, suggests that large corpora should be built incrementally by combining smaller representative samples of sub-languages. It is therefore not necessarily the size of the corpus that is paramount to closure, but the choice of texts within it.

cluster

1. A term used to describe any group of words in sequence (for example as used in **WordSmith Tools**). Also referred to as *lexical bundles* (Biber et al. 1999: 993–4).
2. A set of texts which statistically share similar linguistic features. See **cluster analysis**.

cluster analysis Clustering is the grouping of similar objects (Willett 1988) and a cluster analysis is a multivariate statistical technique that allows the production of categories by purely automatic means (Oakes 1998: 95). Clustering can therefore be used in order to calculate degrees of similarity or difference between multiple texts, based upon criteria set by the researcher. While clustering techniques have a useful application in document retrieval (van Rijsbergen 1979), Oakes (*ibid*.: 110) also notes that in **corpus linguistics** various identifiable features such as case, voice or choice of preposition within a text may be clustered in order to demonstrate how such features are used across different **genres** or by different authors.

CMU Pronouncing Dictionary A machine-readable pronouncing dictionary covering 125,000 words of American English. The resource is mainly of interest to researchers working in the areas of speech recognition and synthesis. See http://www.speech.cs.cmu.edu/cgi-bin/cmudict for details and to download the dictionary.

COALA A **tool** developed in the 1990s that is used for the 'semi-automatic' analysis of **second language acquisition corpora**. See Pienemann (1992).

COBUILD Corpus See **Bank of English**. Also known as the **Birmingham Corpus**.

COCOA Reference A form of text encoding consisting of a pair of angle brackets < > which contain a code standing for a particular type of information and the value assigned to the code. For example, when encoding speech a code such as <pause 2> could be used to show a pause which lasts for a duration of two seconds. COCOA was an early computer program used for extracting indices of words in context from machine-readable texts. Its conventions were carried forward into several other programs, notably the **Oxford Concordance Program (OCP)**. The Longman–Lancaster corpus and the **Helsinki Corpus** have also used COCOA references. There is, however, no clear definition of the syntax of COCOA tagging. In **Standard Generalised Markup Language (SGML)** a slightly more complex version of COCOA references is defined in which the references are referred to as 'elements'.

Codes for the Human Analysis of Transcripts (CHAT) System An **encoding** system that has been developed to be compatible with the analysis program **CLAN** for use with the **Child Language Data Exchange System (CHILDES)** corpus.

cognates Words in different languages that are similar, either in their orthographic or phonetic form, so that it is highly likely that one is a translation of the other. As Simard et al. (1992) have shown, cognates can be useful in aiding sentence **alignment** techniques when working with bilingual or **multilingual corpora**.

Collaborative International Dictionary of English (CIDE) A freely available dictionary based upon a combination of the 1913 Webster's dictionary and definitions from Wordnet. This dictionary is being maintained and proof-read by volunteers from across the world. Different copies are held internationally and a number of inter-faces are available to access the dictionary. GCIDE is one of these variants, being a version of CIDE available from the GNU project. See http://ftp.gnu.org/gnu/gcide/.

colligation A form of **collocation** which involves relation-ships at the grammatical rather than the lexical level. For example, nouns tend to colligate with adjectives while verbs tend to colligate with adverbs. We can also apply colligation to phrases or words. For example, as the examples in Table 2 show, a word like *window* tends to colligate with prepositions.

Table 2. Sample concordance of *window*

prepositional phrase	colligating word	prepositional phrase
ith someone coming in **through** her	window	.
The sun was shining **through** the	window	and illuminated them.
I stood **at** the	window	and looked **down into** the street.
on got up and went **over to** the back	window	.
She padded **across to** the	window	, drew back the curtains and looked
at casual passers-by, looking **in** the	window	**at** the menu, would be more likely t
I can see him **from** the kitchen	window	you see.
was a window and **out through** the	window	she could see down a long tunnel
He found that it opened a	window	**on** the City that he would otherwise
The World **Outside** My	window	encompasses an unusually broad ra

collocation Described by Firth (1957: 14) as 'actual words in habitual company', collocation is the phenomenon surrounding the fact that certain words are more likely to occur in combination with other words in certain contexts. A collocate is therefore a word which occurs within the neighbourhood of another word. For example, within **WordSmith** users can specify a window within which collocational frequencies can be calculated. Table 3 shows the top ten collocates for the word *time* in the **Brown Corpus**, within a −5 to +5 span (the most common collocational position is emboldened for each word):

Table 3. Top ten collocates for 'time'

Word	Total	Left	Right	L5	L4	L3	L2	L1	R1	R2	R3	R4	R5
the	1267	753	514	103	80	60	254	**256**	47	146	100	111	110
and	400	191	209	45	**63**	36	28	19	61	36	35	43	34
for	287	185	102	24	28	**85**	48	0	35	23	13	16	15
that	219	130	89	13	15	25	9	**68**	27	12	10	19	21
was	210	83	127	24	16	27	12	4	21	30	**31**	22	23
this	181	145	36	7	14	5	4	**115**	6	10	8	8	4
had	119	57	62	13	9	16	9	10	6	**20**	14	9	13
his	107	47	60	16	7	4	8	12	2	**18**	11	16	13
same	103	100	3	1	0	3	1	**95**	0	0	0	1	2
from	96	78	18	2	5	25	19	**27**	2	4	2	6	4

Such tables tend to elicit **high-frequency** function words, which although useful, does not always show an exclusive relationship between two words. For example, *the* occurs as a collocate next to many other words, as well as *time*. We would perhaps find lower-frequency lexical words such as *waste*, *devote*, *spend*, *spare* and *limit* to be more illustrative collocates of *time*. **Corpus linguistics** techniques have therefore allowed researchers to demonstrate the frequency *and* exclusivity of particular collocates, using statistical methods such as **mutual information**, the **Z-score** (Berry-Rogghe 1973), MI3 (Oakes 1998: 171-2), log-log (Kilgarriff and Tugwell 2001) or **log-likelihood** (Dunning 1993) scores. Each method returns a value showing strength of collocation, but their criteria for assigment differ. For example, mutual information foregrounds the frequency with which collocates occur together as opposed to their independent occurrence whereas it is more probable that log-likelihood will register strong collocation when the individual words are themselves frequent. So mutual information will give a high collocation score to relatively low-frequency word pairs like *bits/bobs*, whereas log-likelihood will give a higher score to higher-frequency pairs such as *school/teacher*.

Collocations can be useful in terms of language teaching – making students aware of low-frequency collocates that native speakers have internalised (e.g. Hoffman and Lehmann 2000). In addition, collocates can be useful for demonstrating the existence of bias or connotation in words. For example, the strongest collocate in the **British National Corpus (BNC)** of the word *bystander* is *innocent*, suggesting that even in cases where *bystander* occurs without this collocate, the concept of innocence could still be implied. (See also **upward collocation, downward collocation, colligation.**)

common core hypothesis The theory that all varieties of English have central fundamental properties in common with each other, which differ quantitatively rather than qualitatively (Quirk et al. 1985). McEnery and Wilson (1996: 109) suggest that such a theory can be tested using **corpora** and corpus techniques.

comparative linguistics Corpora have been used in comparative linguistics from as early as 1940 when Eaton carried out a study comparing the frequencies of word meanings in Dutch, French, German and Italian. (See also **parallel corpus.**)

competence–performance A dichotomy of language. Competence (or I-language) consists of our tacit internalised knowledge of language, whereas performance (or E-language) is our behaviour in real life. Competence both explains and characterises a speaker's knowledge of a language. Performance, however, is a poor mirror of competence. For example, factors diverse as short-term memory limitations or whether or not we have been drinking alcohol can alter how we speak on any particular occasion. Chomsky (1968: 88) argues that performance data is therefore degenerate. He also argues that corpus data (which is by nature performance data) is a poor guide to modelling linguistic competence. However, Labov (1969) offers a different view, claiming that 'the great majority of utterances in all contexts are grammatical'. Corpus data may therefore not provide us with a perfect model of grammatical competence, but with that said it should also provide cases where performance is not ideal, helping to explain why the competence–performance dichotomy exists. (See also Ingram (1989: 223).)

compilation

'Compiling a corpus means an endless series of compromises' (Rissanen 1992: 188).

A number of stages go into the compilation of a **corpus** (as outlined by Kennedy 1998: 70–85). These include:

1. Corpus **design**: in general, compilers should assume that their corpus will be used for comparative purposes, although the design of the corpus will ultimately be dependent on the sorts of research questions that are being asked.
2. Planning a storage system and keeping records: particularly for spoken conversations it is important to note who was present, the relationships between participants, the topic and degree of formality.

3. Obtaining permission: copyright law and the rights of individuals to confidentiality must be observed.
4. Text capture: written text can be typed by hand, obtained in electronic form (for example via CD-ROM or website) or scanned. Spoken text normally must be transcribed by hand, using clear conventions to represent prosodic phenomena.
5. Markup: conventions for indicating text features such as line breaks, line numbers, chapters, paragraphs etc. can be encoded, preferably using a recognised standard such as the **Text Encoding Initiative (TEI)** which is an application of **Standard Generalised Markup Language (SGML)**.

Compleat Lexical Tutor A **data-driven learning**, web-based program developed by Tom Cobb at the University of Montreal. It is designed to assist in **L2** language acquisition. The site is of interest to L2 learners of English, French and Spanish. See http://132.208.224.131/.

Complete Corpus of Old English A corpus of 3,022 surviving Old English texts prepared at the University of Toronto and published in 1981. The corpus was used as the basis for the *Dictionary of Old English*.

compliant A **corpus**, text, tool or **annotation** scheme is compliant with a standard if it follows all the recommendations laid down in that standard. For example, if a text's **SGML/XML** encoding fits with the rules of the **Text Encoding Initiative (TEI)**, it may be described as *TEI compliant*. If a **part-of-speech tagset** adheres to the structure for tagsets recommended in the **EAGLES** Guidelines, it is EAGLES compliant.

compound noun A series of two or more nouns which generally function as a single noun. Compound nouns can be closed, when the words are melded together (e.g. *keyboard*), hyphenated (*sky-scraper*) or open (*mineral water*). Researchers have employed **corpus**-based analysis to identify compound nouns. See Kobayasi et al. (1994), Pustejovsky et al. (1993).

computational linguistics A field of linguistics which involves the scientific study of language from a computational perspective. This often involves the synthesis of computer science, artificial intelligence and linguistic theory. Computational models of linguistic phenomena are created by using knowledge-based or data-driven techniques and **corpora** have been particularly useful in enabling the creation of data-driven models. Computational linguists work on problems such as **machine translation**, **information retrieval**, speech recognition and synthesis, voice response systems, web search engines, text editors, language instruction manuals and automated content analysis.

computer aided grammar instruction An application for annotated **corpora**. Increasingly frequently, a computer program is used to teach grammatical analysis to students of languages and linguistics. Often, these programs exploit corpora with **part-of-speech tagging** or **parsing**. The computer offers the student a sentence, which they annotate; the student's effort is then compared to the tagging in the corpus, and the student can receive instant feedback. The large size of many corpora means a very large number of sentences is available to the student to practise on. (See also **Computer Assisted Language Learning (CALL)**.)

Computer Archive of Modern English Texts (CAMET) An

organisation founded by Geoffrey Leech in 1970 at Lancaster University. CAMET was responsible for creating the **Lancaster/Oslo–Bergen (LOB) corpus**. In 1984, CAMET was transformed into **UCREL**.

Computer Assisted Language Learning (CALL) The use of computers to aid or support the learning of language (**L1** or **L2**). Earlier examples of CALL included 'drill master' or 'quiz master' approaches to programmed instruction, while more recent techniques have favoured the use of **concordances** in the classroom where the student takes a more active role as a 'language detective' or researcher; see Tribble and Jones (1990) and Murison-Bowie (1993). (See also **computer aided grammar instruction, data-driven learning, language teaching.**)

Computerized Language Analysis (CLAN) System A set of thirty-eight computer programs designed to carry out data analyses, used with files from the **Child Language Data Exchange System (CHILDES)**. It includes several searching tools as well as parsers in twelve languages.

ConcApp A freeware, Windows-based, **concordance** application (ConcApp) developed by Chris Greaves at the Polytechnic University of Hong Kong. The system is available for downloading from: http://www.edict. com.hk/PUB/concapp/. Version 4 of the program is **Unicode compliant** and can process most writing systems.

concordance Also referred to as **key word in context (KWIC)**, a concordance is a list of all of the occurrences of a particular search term in a **corpus,** presented within the context in which they occur – usually a few words to the left and right of the search term. A search term is often a single word although many concordance programs allow users to search on multiword phrases, words containing wildcards, tags or combinations of words and tags. Concordances can usually be **sorted** alphabetically on either the search term itself or to x places left or right of the search term, allowing linguistic patterns to be more easily observed by humans. As with **collocation**s, concordances provide information about the 'company that a word keeps'. For example, Table 4 shows a **thinned** concordance of the word *witnessed* sorted one place to the right (the sorted token is marked in bold print).

Table 4. Sample concordance of *witnessed*

1	y told Tom Jones that he had never before	witnessed	**a** Cabinet scene like it." All who were
2	the early decades of the twentieth century	witnessed	**an** increase in the power of medical m
3	uld be drawn up carefully and signed and	witnessed	**in** a particular way. If you write it
4	The first attitude has been	witnessed	**in** the 1930s and during our more rece
5	nk had recovered from the breakdown we	witnessed	**in** late 1986 and, despite the months al
6	fought essentially on national issues and it	witnessed	**the** return not only of a reforming Libe
7	The last year of Ayliffe's Presidency	witnessed	**the** fulfilment of one of the BDDA's ea
8	eneration after the coming of Cyrus which	witnessed	**the** most brilliant speculations of the "
9	dirt, gloom and misery as I never before	witnessed	". Queen Victoria had the curtains of h
10	ood that this small Year Niner has been "	witnessed	" to and moves on to his next victim.

Even in this small sample it is possible to note patterns – *witnessed* tends to precede an article or the preposition *in*. The concordance also shows different meanings of *witnessed*, from a legal usage in line 3 (*signed and witnessed*), to a meaning to do with noting a remarkable event as in line 8 (*witnessed the most brilliant specu-lations*). The phrase *never before witnessed* occurs twice in the concordance (lines 1 and 9), also suggesting that *witnessed* is often used to denote a remarkable or unusual event.

As many concordance searches can produce hundreds or thousands of lines, Sinclair (1999) advocates selecting 30 random lines and noting patterns in them, then select-ing a different 30, noting the new patterns, and so on until a further selection of 30 lines reveals nothing new.

Concordance (R. J. C. Watt) This Windows-based **concord-ance** program developed by R. J. C. Watt of Dundee University, UK, is available for purchase on the web. It includes a range of standard concordance functions. The program has the ability to work with a number of East Asian writing systems as well as those using the Roman alphabet, though the program is not currently **Unicode compliant**. See http://www.concordancesoftware.co.uk/.

concordancer A software **tool** that searches through a **corpus** for each instance of a given word, phrase or other element and the immediate context in which each instance occurs, to create a **concordance**.

Concordancer/Le Concordanceur (D. W. Rand) A freeware **concordance** program for the Macintosh computer, authored by D. W. Rand of the University of Montreal. The program offers basic concordancing features. See http://www.crm.umontreal.ca/~rand/CC_an.html.

consistency In **corpus annotation** consistency can be a prob-lematic issue. Annotation is said to be *consistent* if the same phenomenon is always annotated in the same way throughout the corpus. Unfortunately, there is sufficient **ambiguity** in language that there are often cases where more than one analysis is possible. For instance, in English the word *what* when occurring at the start of certain sorts of clauses can be considered to be *either* a conjunction *or* a pronoun (as for instance in *he asked me what I wanted*). If more than one person is involved in adding part-of-speech tags to a corpus there is a risk that they will make different decisions in borderline cases like this. This would result in inconsistent annotation. To avoid this, it is often necessary to compile a lengthy manual for any annotation scheme, recording and standardising all decisions made in the debatable cases. Even so, inconsistencies may remain. They can be uncovered using an *inter-annotator consistency test*, where different analysts annotate the same text independently, to check that they are annotating the text in the same way.

Consortium for Lexical Research (CLR) The CLR was established in 1991 under the Directorship of Yorick Wilks at the Computing Research Laboratory of New Mexico State University. The aim of the CLR was to develop an **archive** of sharable natural language resources. The consortium stopped accepting new members in the mid-1990s, at which time it also stopped accepting new resources for deposit. However, it did also then open up the majority of its existing holdings to non-members. These resources remain available to the research community. See http://clr.nmsu.edu/cgi-bin/Tools/CLR/clrcat for a catalogue of the material available from the CLR.

Constituent Likelihood Automatic Word-tagging System (CLAWS) CLAWS is a **part-of-speech tagger** developed by **UCREL** at Lancaster University. It was used to tag the

British National Corpus. The system has adopted an approach based on **probabilistic disambiguation,** rather than one based purely on grammatical rules. Such an approach requires prior processing from an existing tagged **corpus** in order to discover the statistical probabilities of the occurrence of different linguistic elements. CLAWS has consistently achieved 96–7 per cent **accuracy** (the precise degree of accuracy varying according to the type of text). Corpus-based tagging with CLAWS therefore consists of three stages: pre-edit, automatic tag assignment and manual **post-edit**. A number of tagsets have been used with CLAWS at different times – the C7 **tagset** consists of almost 140 tags, while the tagset used for the BNC, the C5 tagset, contains just over sixty tags. See Garside (1987, 1996) and Garside and Smith (1997). A web-based CLAWS trial-service is available from: http://www.comp.lancs. ac.uk/computing/research/ucrel/claws/.

Constraint Grammar Parser of English (ENGCG) A combined **part-of-speech tagger** and parser developed at the University of Helsinki. The **part-of-speech tagging** is used as the basis for **parsing,** with the entire process consisting of progressive **rule-based disambiguation** through a series of seven modules. The parser employs a dependency grammar analysis. The system works using the Constraint Grammar formalism and has been used to annotate the **Bank of English**. Karlsson (1994) reports an error rate of 0.3 per cent for word-class tagging of the 94–7 per cent of words that are given an unambiguous tag, whereas with parsing 3 per cent of the words are given an incorrect label and only 85 per cent are assigned a single tag. See Karlsson et al. (1995) for more details of this tagger. (See also http://www.lingsoft.fi/cgi-bin/ engcg.)

content words A set of words in a language consisting of nouns, adjectives, main verbs and adverbs. When measures of **lexical density** are calculated on a text or **corpus**, sometimes only the content words are taken into account. (See also **function words, lexical richness**.)

conversation analysis Spoken **corpora** such as the **London–Lund Corpus (LLC)** of spoken English, the spoken section of the **British National Corpus (BNC)** and the **Bergen Corpus of London Teenage Language (COLT)** have been used in order to facilitate the analysis of conversations. Many of these studies are **corpus-based** rather than **corpus-driven** and have focused on words and phrases which are frequently found in spoken conversations. For example, Stenström (1984) correlated discourse items such as *well, sort of* and *you know* with pauses in speech and showed that such correlations related to whether or not the speaker expects a response from the addressee. Another study by Stenström (1987) examined 'carry-on signals' such as *right, right-o* and *all right* which were classified according to their various functions. Aijmer (2002) has also examined discourse particles such as *now, just* and *actually* in spoken corpora.

Cooperative, Coordinated Natural Language Utterances (Coconut) Corpus Developed by the Coconut project at the University of Pittsburgh, this **corpus** consists of a number of human–human computer mediated dialogues. Pairs of human participants were set the task of deciding what furniture to buy for a house. The resulting typed dialogue was recorded and it is these dialogues which make up the Coconut Corpus. The corpus is made up of twenty-four such dialogues, some of which include dialogue annotation. See Di Eugenio et al. (1998) for more details of the corpus and annotation scheme. (See also http://www.pitt.edu/~coconut/coconut-corpus. html.)

copyright The right to publish and sell literary, musical or artistic work. **Corpus** compilers need to observe copyright law by ensuring that they seek permission from the relevant copyright holders to include particular texts. This can often be a difficult and time-consuming process as copyright ownership is not always clear – some texts are owned by the publisher, while others are owned by the author. If the corpus is likely to be made publicly available, copyright holders may require a fee for allowing their text(s) to be included, particularly if the corpus is believed to hold commercial value. Kennedy (1998: 77) notes that if permission is sought, many copyright holders are willing to facilitate genuine research by allowing their texts to appear in a corpus.

corpora see **corpus**

corpus The word *corpus* is Latin for body (plural *corpora*). In linguistics a corpus is a collection of texts (a 'body' of language) stored in an electronic database. Corpora are usually large bodies of machine-readable text containing thousands or millions of words. A corpus is different from an **archive** in that often (but not always) the texts have been selected so that they can be said to be representative of a particular language variety or genre, therefore acting as a standard reference. Corpora are often annotated with additional information such as **part-of-speech tags** or to denote prosodic features associated with speech. Individual texts within a corpus usually receive some form of meta-encoding in a **header**, giving information about their genre, the author, date and place of publication etc. Types of corpora include **specialised, reference, multilingual, parallel, learner, diachronic** and **monitor**. Corpora can be used for both quantitative and qualitative analyses. Although a corpus does not contain new information about language, by using software packages which process data we can obtain a new perspective on the familiar (Hunston 2002: 2–3).

corpus-based Tognini-Bonelli (2001) makes a useful distinction between corpus-based and corpus-driven investigations. The former uses a **corpus** as a source of examples to check researcher intuition or to examine the **frequency** and/or plausibility of the language contained within a smaller **data** set. The researcher does not question pre-existing traditional descriptive units and categories. A corpus-driven analysis is a more inductive process: the corpus itself is the data and the patterns in it are noted as a way of expressing regularities (and exceptions) in language. A corpus-driven analysis tends to only use minimal theoretical presuppositions about grammatical structure.

Corpus del Español A 100-million-word **corpus** of Spanish created by Mark Davies of Brigham Young University, USA. The corpus is a **diachronic** collection of Spanish from the thirteenth century to the present day. The present-day material includes both written and spoken Spanish. The corpus has been **part-of-speech tagged** and can be queried on-line. See http://www.corpusdelespanol.org/ to access the corpus and see Davies (2000) for more details of the corpus.

corpus-driven see **corpus-based**

Corpus Encoding Standard (CES) Part of the **Expert Advisory Group on Language Engineering (EAGLES)** Guidelines. It sets out a system for the **Standard Generalised Markup Language (SGML) encoding** of **corpus** texts, and provides a **document type definition (DTD)** for encoding written **corpora**. This defines many of the SGML elements most commonly used in corpora, such as <p> for paragraph, <div> for division, and so on. The CES is closely compatible with the **Text Encoding Initiative (TEI)** recommendations. A version created in 2002, XCES, implements the Corpus Encoding Standard as an **XML** application. See http://www.cs.vassar.edu/ CES/.

corpus linguistics A scholarly enterprise concerned with the compilation and analysis of **corpora** (Kennedy 1998: 1). According to McEnery and Wilson (1996: 1) it is the 'study of language based on examples of "real life" language use' and 'a methodology rather than an aspect of language requiring explanation or description'. Stubbs (1996: 231), in noting the relative youth of corpus linguistics, argues that it 'has as yet only very preliminary outlines of a theory which can relate individual texts to text corpora'. Early (**pre-electronic**) studies which used large bodies of text to analyse language included diary studies of child language (Preyer 1889, Stern 1924), research into language pedagogy (Fries and Traver 1940, Bongers 1947), spelling conventions (Käding 1897) and **comparative linguistics** (Eaton 1940). However, in a series of influential publications, Chomsky (1957, 1965) helped to change the direction of linguistics away from **empiricism** and towards rationalism. Although some **corpus-based** work was carried out in the 1960s (for instance Quirk's work on the **Survey of English Usage** (1960) and Francis and

Kučera's work on the **Brown Corpus** (1964)), it was not until the 1980s, with advances in the availability of institutional and private computing facilities, that corpus linguistics began to grow and be accepted as a valid means of language enquiry. The main ways that **corpus data** can be manipulated via software packages, according to Hunston (2002: 3), are to show **frequency, phrase structure** and **collocation**.

Corpus of Early American English Designed as a supplement to the **Helsinki Corpus of English Texts,** the Corpus of Early American English represents the period from about 1620 to 1720 when the foundations of the first overseas variety of English were being laid down. See Kytö (1992).

Corpus of Early English Correspondence (CEEC) Approximately 2.7 million words of English taken from written correspondence of the period 1410–1681, produced by the historical sociolinguistics team at the Research Unit for Variation and Change in English at the University of Helsinki. The **corpus** contains around 6,000 letters written by 778 informants, roughly twenty per cent of whom were female. A subset of the corpus is also available. This **sample corpus** is 450,000 words in size, covering the period 1418–1680, and contains 1,147 letters from 194 informants. See Keränen (1998) for more details. (See also http://www.eng.helsinki.fi/varieng/team2/1_2_4_projects.htm.)

Corpus of English-Canadian Writing Created at Queens University in Kingston, Ontario, the Corpus of English-Canadian Writing contains the same written **genre** categories as the Brown family of **corpora**, with additional categories for feminism and computing. It is also designed to be three times as large as the **Brown Corpus** (that is, to contain 3 million words of Canadian English).

Corpus of Late Eighteenth-Century Prose A **corpus** of around 300,000 words of English from the period 1761–1789 developed at the University of Manchester by a team led by David Denison. The documents included in the corpus are letters, mainly focused upon practical subjects. The corpus is **marked up** in a format identical to the **Helsinki Corpus**, though an **HTML** version of the corpus is also available. See Denison (1994) or http://www.art.man.ac.uk/english/staff/dd/ lmodeprs.htm for further details.

Corpus of Middle English Prose and Verse A **corpus** of sixty-one Middle English texts developed by the Humanities Text Initiative, University of Michigan, USA. The corpus is marked up according to the **Text Encoding Initiative** (**TEI**) guidelines. It may be downloaded or can be searched via an on-line search facility. See http://www. hti.umich.edu/c/cme/.

Corpus Resources and Terminology Extraction (CRATER) CRATER is a **parallel corpus** consisting of documents in English, Spanish and French. The **corpus** contains a million words of text in each language (and more in English and French) from the International Tele-communications Union (ITU). The texts are **lemmatised**, **part-of-speech tagged** and **aligned** at the sentence level. The corpus is available at http://www.comp.lancs.ac.uk/ linguistics/crater/corpus.html.

Corpus of Spoken American English (CSAE) Also referred to as the Santa Barbara Corpus of Spoken American English, the CSAE is the first large electronic **corpus** of spoken American English as used by adults. It is based on hundreds of recordings of naturally occurring speech from across the United States representing a wide variety of people from different regions, social and ethnic backgrounds. See Chafe et al. (1991).

Corpus of Spoken Professional American English A **corpus** constructed from a selection of transcripts of interactions in professional settings, containing two main sub-**corpora** of 1 million words each. One sub-corpus consists mainly of academic discussions such as faculty council meetings and committee meetings related to testing. The second sub-corpus contains transcripts of White House press conferences, which are almost exclusively question-and-answer sessions (cf. Barlow 1998). The corpus is available with and without **part-of-speech annotation** for a modest fee. See http://www.athel.com/cspatg.html.

Corpus of Written British Creole (CWBC) A 12,000-word **corpus** containing written texts of English-lexicon Caribbean Creole (Patois/Patwa/Nation Language) consisting of poems, extracts from novels, plays, advertisements and graffiti. The corpus is **annotated** to show spelling, grammatical and discourse information.

corpus sampler Many large **corpus**-building projects also produce a smaller sample taken from the completed corpus, usually offered free of charge, to be used in situations in which millions of words of data are not required. The sampler can be used, for example, as a **training corpus** or as a comparative corpus when producing **keywords**.

Corpus Wizard A shareware **concordance** package by

Hamagushi Takahashi. The **concordancer** is written for the Windows and OS/2 operating systems. The program provides a range of basic concordancing functions. It is not **Unicode compliant**. For further details see http://www2d.biglobe.ne.jp/~htakashi/software/cw2e.htm.

Cronfa Electroneg o Gymraeg (CEG) A 1,079,032-word corpus of modern Welsh. The corpus loosely follows the **Brown Corpus** sampling frame, though the sampling period for the corpus was quite loose with many, but not all, texts sampled post-1970. More details of the corpus can be found at http://www.bangor.ac.uk/ar/cb/ceg/ceg_eng.html.

D

data Information of any kind. Specifically, in **corpus linguistics**, *data* is the text contained in **corpora,** so we may speak of 'a million words of spoken data' etc. Data may also refer to statistics, **concordances** or **collocations** extracted from corpora.

Natural language data is text which has been produced in the 'real world'. *Artificial data* is any language data which is not natural. (See also **attested data, modified data, intuitive data.**)

data-driven learning Sometimes also referred to as 'discovery learning', this is a technique devised by Tim Johns (1997), used in **language teaching** whereby the student takes a pro-active role in their own learning process by carrying out and analysing a series of **concordances** from a corpus. The advantage of data-driven learning is that it should help to increase student motivation, particularly when the search is prompted by their own questions.

Such activities can be directed by a teacher (who already knows what the results of the concordance analysis will bring), or can be carried out alone. However, as Hunston (2002: 171) points out, the former would require the teacher to carry out advance preparation while the latter may result in unpredictable outcomes. As Bernadini (2000) shows, data-driven learning is likely to be most useful to very advanced learners for filling in gaps in their knowledge.

database The term 'database' may be used to refer to a large collection of texts. Unlike **corpora**, databases are not made up of samples but instead constitute an entire population of data – for example, the complete works of Thomas Hardy, or all of the editions of the *Guardian* newspaper in a single year. Kennedy (1998: 4) notes that while many large databases are not subjected to corpus analysis, there is no reason why they should not be used for this purpose. Databases include the **Oxford Text Archive (OTA)**, **Acquilex**, **Bellcore**, the **CELEX Relational Database** and **CHILDES**. (See also **archive**.)

design Design is the first of five stages in corpus **compilation** (the others being planning a storage system, obtaining permissions, text collection and **encoding**). The design of a corpus is dependent on the purposes for which it is going to be used, therefore careful thought should be given to the type, content, structure and size of the corpus. Such decisions as whether to include spoken and/or written texts, whether to build a **diachronic** or **synchronic corpus**, which **genres** to include and how large the corpus should be may all figure in the design process. Maintaining a sampled balance of texts in order to achieve an ideal representation of a language variety is desirable, although as many corpus compilers have discovered, not always possible. In addition, texts do not always fit easily into previously created categories. Therefore, building a smaller pilot corpus is a useful way of resolving problematic cases at an early stage. Atkins et al. (1992: 7–9) list text origin, participants, medium, genre, style, setting, factuality, topic, date of publication, authorship, age and intended audience of readership as some of the most important extra-linguistic variables which should be taken into account when considering the content and structure of a corpus.

diachronic corpus A **corpus** that has been carefully built in order to be representative of a language or language variety over a particular period of time, so that it is possible for researchers to track linguistic changes within it. For example, the **Helsinki Corpus of English Texts: Diachronic Part** consists of 400 samples of texts covering the period from AD 750 to 1700 (Kytö and Rissanen 1992). (See also **monitor corpus, synchronic corpus.**)

Diachronic Corpus of Present-day Spoken English (DCPSE) A **corpus** being constructed at the Survey of English Usage, University College London by a team led by Bas Aarts. The corpus includes **spoken corpus data** drawn from both the **London–Lund Corpus** and the spoken section of the British **International Corpus of English (ICE) corpus** in order to develop a **diachronic corpus** of relatively contemporary spoken English covering a period of a quarter of a century or so from the 1960s and early 1990s. The corpus is available from http://www.ucl.ac.uk/english-usage/diachronic/.

dialect corpus A specialised **spoken corpus** (although written texts can also contain dialects), which is compiled in order to carry out studies of regional variation. Speakers in the **corpus** may be categorised according to their dialect, and an **encoding** scheme which distinguishes between variant pronunciations is likely to be employed. (See also **regional corpus, non-standard corpus**.)

Dialogue Annotation Tool (DAT) Developed at the Department of Computer Science, University of Rochester, USA, this tool is designed to apply the DAMSL **markup** scheme to **corpus** texts. DAMSL (discourse act markup in several layers) allows for the **annotation** of multiple layers of information relevant to the understanding and analysis of spontaneous conversation. For more details of DAT, see http://www.cogsci.ed.ac.uk/~amyi/mate/dat.html. For information on DAMSL see http://www.cs.rochester.edu/research/cisd/resources/damsl/Revised Manual/RevisedManual.html.

Dialogue Diversity Corpus A **corpus** of fifty-four dialogues available free of charge for academic research developed by William C. Mann at the University of Southern California, USA. The dialogues are taken from a range of sources and represent a wide range of different interaction types, for example academic discussion, doctor–patient interaction, transaction. All of the dialogues are in English, with most being in American English, though the corpus contains examples of other English varieties also. To download the corpus and for more details see http://www-rcf.usc.edu/~billmann/diversity/DDivers-site.htm.

dictionaries There is a strong relationship between dictionaries and **corpora**. Many dictionaries are now created with the help of **corpus data,** for instance *The Longman*

Dictionary of Contemporary English (*LDOCE*) includes over a million examples of language use from corpus data and gives information about the top 3,000 words in spoken and written English. Dictionaries have also been published in electronic form – for example, the *Oxford English Dictionary* (second edition) on CD-ROM contains more than half a million entries and 2.4 million quotations. Dictionaries themselves have been used as specialised corpora, particularly for automatic sense disambiguation, while a number of lexical **databases** such as the **MRC Psycholinguistic Database**, the **CELEX Relational Database** and the **Acquilex Project** are recommended by Edwards (1993: 296) as being potentially useful for **corpus linguistics** research.

disambiguation Disambiguation is the resolution of **ambiguity** in language. Specifically, in the field of **corpus annotation**, disambiguation refers to a process where the correct annotation is chosen from a set of possible tags at a given point in the text. This may be done manually or automated. Many approaches to **part-of-speech tagging** are centred on disambiguation. First, each **token** in the corpus is assigned all the tags it can possibly have in any context, by looking it up in a tagging **lexicon** or using a **morphological analyser**. Then, disambiguation software uses the context to select the correct tag. Disambiguation is most often accomplished either by means of **rule-based disambiguation** or by a **probabilistic** approach, usually based on a **hidden Markov model**.

discourse prosody A term reported by Tognini-Bonelli (1996) and Stubbs (2001) relating to the way that words in a **corpus** can **collocate** with a related set of words or phrases, often revealing (hidden) attitudes. For example, in the **British National Corpus (BNC)** the word *happen* has a discourse prosody for unpleasant things (see the sample **concordance** in Table 5).

Table 5. Concordance table showing discourse prosody of the word *happen*

le who foresee airplane disasters before they	happen	are said to have this gift.
experience very few genuine disasters ever	happen	in the school playground.
It is a dreadful thing to	happen	."
Luckily, it was the worst thing to	happen	to poor Sal all weekend.
And an accident can	happen	anywhere, at any time just when you least e
I don't want that disaster to	happen	."
Everything you feared might	happen	, did happen, only worse.
Did something terrible	happen	to those verbally adept young girls as they
SIR – Drug poisoning can	happen	in unexpected ways.
ever they lost their car keys, which seemed to	happen	quite frequently.

Stubbs suggests that the difference between **semantic preference** and discourse prosody is not always clear cut; a deciding factor could be to do with how open-ended the list of possible collocates are. He also notes that discourse prosodies could be referred to as pragmatic prosodies. (See also **semantic prosody**.)

dispersion The rate of occurrence of a word or phrase across a particular file or corpus. Dispersion is normally calculated in mathematics using a descriptive statistic like the standard deviation, which gives a measure of the dispersion of a data set in relation to the mean value of the data. In **WordSmith**, a visual representation of the dispersion of a word or phrase can be obtained via a dispersion plot. This enables researchers to determine whether a term is equally spread throughout a text or occurs as a central theme in one or more parts of the text. The following two dispersion plots are both from a small corpus of newsletters produced by a Catholic church. The two words (*joy* and *abortion*) have equal frequencies in the corpus, although the dispersion plots show that the term *joy* is more evenly dispersed throughout the speeches, whereas *abortion* occurs in fewer files and as a more focussed subject of discussion at various points:

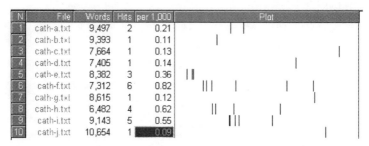

N	File	Words	Hits	per 1,000	Plot
1	cath-a.txt	9,497	2	0.21	
2	cath-b.txt	9,393	1	0.11	
3	cath-c.txt	7,664	1	0.13	
4	cath-d.txt	7,405	1	0.14	
5	cath-e.txt	8,382	3	0.36	
6	cath-f.txt	7,312	6	0.82	
7	cath-g.txt	8,615	1	0.12	
8	cath-h.txt	6,482	4	0.62	
9	cath-i.txt	9,143	5	0.55	
10	cath-j.txt	10,654	1	0.09	

Fig. 1. Dispersion plot of *joy*

N	File	Words	Hits	per 1,000	Plot
1	cath-h.txt	6,482	7	1.08	
2	cath-c.txt	7,664	7	0.91	
3	cath-i.txt	9,142	6	0.66	
4	cath-f.txt	7,311	2	0.27	
5	cath-g.txt	8,615	1	0.12	
6	cath-b.txt	9,394	1	0.11	
7	cath-j.txt	10,654	1	0.09	

Fig. 2. Dispersion plot of *abortion*

distinctiveness coefficient Any statistical method of identifying lexical items that are most commonly associated with a particular language variety. Johansson (1980) adopts a method of comparing linguistic differences between the **Lancaster–Oslo/Bergen (LOB)** and **Brown corpora** with the following calculation:

$$\frac{Freq.Lob - Freq.Brown}{Freq.Lob + Freq.Brown}$$

Another type of distinctiveness coefficient is the **keyword** function utilised by Scott (1999), which uses either **log-likelihood** or **chi-squared** statistical methods in order to derive lists of words that occur more often in one file or **corpus** when compared against another.

distribution A term with two distinct meanings in **corpus linguistics**:

1. Distribution is a factor in corpus **design** – ensuring that the files included in a **corpus** are drawn from a wide and representative range of text categories or **genres**. The **size** of a corpus needs to be offset against the diversity of sources in order to maintain **representativeness** (Kennedy 1998: 68). Biber's (1990) distribution analysis concluded that the typical number of samples within each **genre** of the **Lancaster–Oslo/Bergen (LOB)** and **London–Lund (LLC) corpora** (between twenty to eighty texts) was adequate for correlation-based analyses of **variation**.

2. Linguistic distribution is one method of corpus analysis that is available to researchers (see also **dispersion**). For example, the written part of the **British National Corpus (BNC)** is subdivided into nine writing genres and it is therefore possible to compare frequencies across these genres. Distributions within spoken language can also be explored, using factors such as the sex, age and social class of speakers. Table 6 shows distributions (given as occurrences per million words) of the synonyms *big* and *large* in the different writing genres in the BNC. *Big* occurs more often in leisure and imaginative domains, whereas *large* is more typical of the sciences.

Table 6. Distribution (per million words of *big* and *large* in different genres in the British National Corpus

	big	large
Leisure	395.8	406.8
Imaginative	341.93	227.44
Arts	284.64	310.86
Commerce and finance	275.85	476.06
Applied science	130.9	549.92
World affairs	115.81	370.36
Natural and pure sciences	99.89	819.44
Belief and thought	94.44	244.41
Social science	92.69	338.12
Total	219.39	377.57

ditto tags A process, usually applied in **part-of-speech tagging**, whereby an idiom is given a single 'tag' spread over several words. For example, consider the sentence 'It happened all of a sudden'. The phrase 'all of a sudden' could be said to function as an adverb. Rather than tagging this phrase with individual parts of speech (for example, all_DET of_PREP a_ART sudden_ADJ) the phrase is considered to be an adverb consisting of four parts and is given ditto tags accordingly: all_ADV41 of_ADV42 a_ADV43 sudden_ADV44. The first of the two numbers at the end of each tag denotes the number of words in the idiom(in this case 4), whereas the second number defines the position of each word in the idiom. Ditto tags are usually specified by **rule-based disambiguation** software. Decisions regarding what constitutes a ditto tag are somewhat subjective and need to be agreed on in advance of tagging and also included in the corpus **documentation**.

documentation A well-constructed **corpus** will usually be released with accompanying documentation, explaining the **design** and **encoding** of the corpus. Information which one would usually expect to find in a corpus manual, as the documentation is often called, might include who built the corpus, and for what purpose, the **size** of the corpus, what texts it contains and how these were sampled. This last might describe the sources of the texts or their **genres**; for a **spoken corpus**, the way the recordings were made and transcribed would be specified. Good corpus documentation will also specify the **character set** used, the **markup** system and any analytic **annotation** that is used in the corpus (including how decisions were made about tagging ambiguities, **ditto tags** etc).

document type definition (DTD) In **Standard Generalised Markup Language (SGML)** and **Extensible Markup Language (XML)**, a DTD is the set of statements that define what **markup** tags are allowed in a text file, what they can contain, and what attributes they can have. The DTD is usually stored in a separate file to the text, so that many text files can use the same DTD and be encoded uniformly.

Because of the great diversity in the structure and contents of corpus texts, the DTDs used in corpus linguistics are typically very complicated, for instance the **Text Encoding Initiative**'s TEI Lite DTD (see http://www.tei-c.org/Lite/DTD/).

downward collocation A form of **collocation** outlined by Sinclair (1991: 115–19) whereby the focus is upon *semantic* patterns surrounding a particular lexical item. Downward collocation occurs when one collocate occurs less frequently in a **corpus** or text than its collocational pair. Downward collocates tend to be **content**

words rather than **function words**. For example, downward collocates of the word *bank* (which occurs 17,596 times in the **British National Corpus**) are *Jodrell* (21 occurrences), *Israeli-occupied* (29), *overdrafts* (78), *lending* (1,307) and *robber* (189). These words suggest two unrelated semantic patterns of *bank* connected to either geographic locations or finance. (See also **upward collocation, semantic preference**.)

duplication In large **corpora**, which are often compiled by a team of several researchers, or even compiled automatically from sources such as the **World Wide Web** or daily newspaper text, there is a risk that some texts will be included twice or more in the corpus. That is, two texts with different labels will actually contain the exact same document. Duplication is, therefore, an important issue for corpus **design**.

Duplication is undesirable because it can distort the apparent **frequency** of very rare words or forms. If a duplicated text contains something that actually only occurs once in a 100-million-word corpus, then it will appear to occur, on average, once every 50 million words – a huge difference.

Sections of text can also be duplicated in a corpus. For instance, many web pages on news sites contain fixed text at the start and end (called **boilerplate**); if the pages are incorporated directly into a corpus, that boilerplate will be included in every document, and have the same distorting effect on statistics derived from the corpus.

dynamic corpus A dynamic corpus is one which is continually growing over time, as opposed to a **static corpus**, which does not change in size once it has been built. Dynamic **corpora** are useful in that they provide the means to monitor language change over time – for this reason they are sometimes referred to as **monitor** corpora. Examples of dynamic corpora include the Longman Written American Corpus and the **Bank of English (BoE)**. The **American National Corpus (ANC)** also has a dynamic component, consisting of texts added at regular intervals to the initial, basic corpus. (See also **diachronic corpus**.)

E

embedded quotes When a quotation contains a quotation, the inner quotation is said to be embedded. For instance, *The man told me, 'my father said "never do that", so I never have.'* The words *never do that* are an embedded quote. Often, when quotes are embedded, alternating double quotation marks ("") and single quotation marks (') are used. Handling embedded quotes is not always straightforward for a computer as quotation marks are typically used to represent the start and end of a **string**.

empiricism An empirical approach to knowledge is based on the idea that knowledge comes from our experiences or from observation of the world. In linguistics, empiricism is the idea that the best way to find out about how language works is by analysing real examples of language as it is actually used. **Corpus linguistics** is therefore a strongly empirical methodology. An approach to knowledge which relies on **introspection** rather than observation is called rationalism, which in the field of linguistics is strongly associated with Noam Chomsky. (See also **corpus linguistics**.)

Enabling Minority Language Engineering (EMILLE) Corpus A **corpus** of South Asian languages constructed as part of a collaborative venture between Lancaster University and the Central Institute of Indian Languages (CIIL), Mysore, India. EMILLE is distributed by **ELRA**. The corpus consists of three components: monolingual, **parallel** and **annotated** corpora. There are monolingual **corpora** for fourteen South Asian languages: Assamese, Bengali, Gujarati, Hindi, Kannada, Kashmiri, Malayalam, Marathi, Oriya, Punjabi, Sinhala, Tamil, Telegu and Urdu. The EMILLE monolingual corpora contain 93 million words (including 2.6 million words of transcribed spoken data for Bengali, Gujarati, Hindi, Punjabi and Urdu). The parallel corpus consists of 200,000 words of text in English and accompanying translations in Bengali, Gujarati, Hindi, Punjabi and Urdu. The annotated component includes the Urdu corpora annotated for **parts-of-speech,** together with twenty written Hindi corpus files annotated to show the nature of demonstrative use. The corpus is encoded as **Unicode** with **CES** compliant **SGML markup**. See Baker et al. (2004).

enclitic A **clitic** that attaches to the end of the previous word. See **proclitic**.

encoding Encoding is usually the last of the five stages of corpus **compilation,** and is sometimes referred to as **annotation, tagging** or **markup**. Encoding is a way of representing elements in texts such as paragraph breaks, utterance boundaries etc. in a standardised way across a **corpus,** so that they can be more easily recognised by computer software and by corpus users.

A number of standardised text encoding schemes are in existence, including the **Text Encoding Initiative (TEI)** which makes use of the **Standard Generalised Markup Language (SGML)** and was used for encoding the **British National Corpus (BNC)**. The **Child Language Data**

Exchange System (CHILDES) database of child language was created using an encoding scheme called **Codes for the Human Analysis of Transcripts (CHAT)** that is formulated for encoding the complexities of spoken **data**.

Annotation can also occur at the meta-linguistic level – for example, by adding information such as author, level of readership or date of publication to a text's **header** – or it can encode an analysis of some feature at the discourse, semantic, grammatical, lexical, morphological or phonetic level. For example, automatic **part-of-speech tagging** can be carried out on a corpus, whereby every word within it is assigned a particular grammatical tag as shown in the following example below:

```
Anyway_AV0 ,_, I_PNP rented_VVD out_AVP a_AT0
few_DT0 horror_NN1 films_NN2 and_CJC am_VBB
coming_VVG to_PRP the_AT0 conclusion_NN1 that_CJT
horror_NN1 films_NN2 are_VBB all_DT0 about_PRP
fears_NN2 of_PRF social_AJ0 class_NN1
```

English–Norwegian Parallel Corpus This **parallel corpus** is made up of original texts in either English or Norwegian together with their translations into the other language. There are thus four sections: original English, translated English, original Norwegian and translated Norwegian. It was designed for use in contrastive analysis and translation studies. It contains both fictional and non-fiction texts and is, in total, about 2.6 million words in size.

English Trigram Frequencies A list of letter trigrams derived from the **Brown Corpus** derived by John Cowan. The list is available at http://home.ccil.org/~cowan/trigrams.

ethics As with other forms of **data** collection for analysis, ethical considerations need to be taken into account for the **compilation** of a **corpus**. Specifically, permission must be obtained from the relevant bodies (usually the author and/or the publisher) for including a written text within a corpus. For spoken or recorded texts, participants must be made aware that they are being recorded in advance, be given the right to have their identities disguised if they wish, be able to give their informed, voluntary consent to being recorded and be allowed access to the recording in order to erase any parts with which they are uncomfortable. Furthermore, the researcher should not use his or her status in order to influence participants. For further information see Seiber (1992) or Homan (1991). The British Association for Applied Linguistics (BAAL) has information at their website entitled *Recommendations on Good Practice in Applied Linguistics*, see http://www.baal.org.uk/goodprac.htm.

Eudico Linguistic Annotator (ELAN) The tool was developed by a team at the Max Planck Institute for Psycholinguistics, Nijmegen specifically to handle multimodal **corpora** in which annotations coexist alongside other types of data such as transcriptions and video streams. The tool both supports the browsing of such corpora and their construction/annotation. The tool is freely available, with versions compliant to both Windows and Macintosh. For more details see http://www.mpi.nl/tools/elan.html.

Euralex The European Association for Lexicography (Euralex) was founded in 1983 with the aim of furthering the field of **lexicography** by promoting the exchange of ideas and information, often across discipline boundaries. **Corpus-based** lexicography is prominent in the areas of interest explored by Euralex members. See http://www.ims.uni-stuttgart.de/euralex/   for   more details of the association, including its conferences.

European Chapter of the Association for Computational Linguistics (EACL) The European wing of the **ACL** was founded in the early 1980s. It organises a conference every three years and is the primary professional organisation in Europe for **computational linguistics**. See http://www.eacl.org.

European Corpus Initiative (ECI) The European Corpus Initiative was founded to create a large multilingual **corpus** for scientific research. The corpus (ECI/MCI) has been available on CD-ROM since 1994. It contains texts in a range of languages including German, French, Spanish, Dutch, Albanian, Chinese, Czech and Malay as well as some **parallel** texts. The corpus is distributed by the European Network of Excellence in Human Language Technologies (ELSNET).

European Language Activity Network (ELAN) A project led by Laurent Romary that was designed to encourage the take-up of language resources, including **corpora,** by the users of such resources. This was achieved via the development of common standards for **data** interchange and engagement in a number of awareness-raising exercises to publicise the existence of language resources. See http://www.loria.fr/projets/MLIS/ELAN/.

European Language Resources Association (ELRA) The European organisation that promotes and oversees the production and distribution of language resources for use in **natural language processing,** and the evaluation of NLP technologies. ELRA organises the LREC series of conferences every two years. Its operational body is the **Evaluations and Language Resources Distribution Agency (ELDA)**.

European Network of Excellence in Human Language Technologies (ELSNET) A multidisciplinary grouping which seeks to bring together all those whose research touches upon **natural language processing**, including **corpus linguists**. The network has a number of special interest groups, with language resources as one of its six main focuses. In addition to providing an infrastructure to connect researchers across discipline boundaries, ELSNET also undertakes trainsing via its summer schools and workshops. See http://www.elsnet.org/.

European Science Foundation Second Language Databank (ESFSLD) A corpus collected by research groups of the European Science Foundation project in France, Germany, Great Britain, the Netherlands and Sweden. The project concentrates on second language acquisition of immigrant workers living in Western Europe, and their communication with native speakers in their respective host countries.

Eustace Corpus see **Centre for Speech Technology Research**

Evaluations and Language Resources Distribution Agency (ELDA) The profit making, commercial counterpart of the **European Language Resources Association (ELRA)**. ELDA works to identify, classify, collect, validate and produce language resources that are used by language technologists. This includes both producing and validating language **corpora**.

Expert Advisory Group on Language Engineering Standards (EAGLES) The EAGLES project ran from 1993 to 1996 under the auspices of the European Union. Its aim was to develop a set of standards (often referred to as the EAGLES Guidelines) in a number of areas of **corpus linguistics** and **natural language processing**. In most cases, the methods recommended by EAGLES were based on approaches and practices that had already developed in common use.

The EAGLES Guidelines cover a number of different aspects of corpus encoding and annotation. There are recommendations on: the classification of different types of **corpora**; the classification of texts in a corpus; the **encoding** of **corpora** (see **Corpus Encoding Standard**); the **tagsets** used to annotate corpora for **part-of-speech** or syntactic structure (see **parsing**); the grammatical information encoded in computational **lexicons**; the evaluation of **NLP** systems and formalisms for computer **grammars**. The guidelines are published at http://www.ilc.cnr.it/EAGLES96/browse.html.

Extensible Markup Language (XML) A **markup** language based on the **Standard Generalised Markup Language (SGML)** that is used for **encoding** electronic texts. In appearance it is very similar to SGML, being based on tags in angled brackets < > which may also contain attribute-value pairs, for instance <div type="chapter"> to indicate one type of text division. Also like SGML, XML defines the tags that can occur in a document, and the structure in which they occur, using a **document type definition (DTD)**.

XML was developed in the 1990s as a more restricted **markup** language than SGML, offering fewer optional features. For example, using SGML it is possible to have tags with no end tag, such as <br> to indicate a line break. In XML this is not allowed, so all tags must either come in pairs (
</br>) or else as a special combined start-and-end tag (<br/>). These restrictions make XML easier to process.

XML is now widely used in **corpus linguistics**, and many of the main SGML applications used to encode **corpora** have been updated to use XML, for instance the **Text Encoding Initiative** and the **Corpus Encoding Standard**.

F

Fidditch Parser Developed by Donald Hindle, this is a computer-based **tool** which carries out automatic **parsing** of texts. It is a non-probabilistic **parser**, working via a series of grammatical rules.

first generation corpora This is a name given to a series of relatively small **corpora** that were created using a similar model. These include the **Brown Corpus** of American English (1961), the **Lancaster–Oslo/Bergen** (LOB) corpus of British English (1961), the **Kolhapur Corpus of Indian English** (1978), the **Wellington Corpus of Written New Zealand English** (1986) and the **Australian Corpus of English** (1986). Although these early corpora have been criticised in terms of their limited size and sampling (see Kennedy 1998: 30), they still continue to be important sources for analysis, as well as acting as models for the **compilation** of further corpora. (See also **second generation corpora**.)

Fisher's Exact Test A test of statistical significance which is more reliable than either the **chi-squared** or **log-likelihood** statistics where the data set under investigation includes low expected frequencies (less than 5). See McEnery, Xiao and Tono (2005).

Floresta Sintá(c)tica A joint Danish/Portuguese project which has produced two **treebanks** of Portuguese. The **corpora** were parsed using a **parser** called Palavras (Bick, 2000). The two corpora are called Bosque and Floresta Virgem. Bosque is a 174,856-word **corpus** containing 8,818 parsed sentences. The output of the parser used to annotate Bosque has been hand corrected. The second corpus, Floresta Virgem, is a 1,072,857-word corpus containing 41,406 sentences. This corpus, while parsed, has not been hand corrected. Both corpora have been built using subsections of previously created corpora of Portuguese. See http://acdc.linguateca.pt/treebank/info_ floresta_English.html for further information, including details of how to access the corpora.

fnTBL A machine-learning toolkit geared towards **natural language processing** tasks such as **part-of-speech tagging**. The toolkit was developed at John Hopkins University, USA, by Radu Florian and Grace Ngai. The software is available to download, free of charge from http://nlp.cs.jhu.edu/~rflorian/fntbl/.

form-focused teaching Form-focused teaching is a method of language teaching whereby the teacher gives explicit form (or grammar) focused instruction as feedback in order to facilitate self-correction. Form-focused teaching may therefore arise in response to a mistake, or a question from a student. A **corpus-based** approach to form-focused teaching would involve the student and/or teacher using a **corpus** to investigate aspects of the student's language use, informing instruction rather than determining it.

Forward–Backward algorithm see **Baum–Welch algorithm**.

Framenet A project based at the University of Berkeley, USA, which is seeking to produce a **corpus-based lexicon** with the needs of language learners, language teachers and lexicographers in mind. The basic ideas behind the project are derived from work in frame semantics (see Fillmore, 1985). For more information about Framenet see http://www.icsi.berkeley.edu/~framenet/.

Freiburg–Brown Corpus of American English (Frown) The Frown Corpus consists of 1 million words of written American English from the early 1990s. The text categories, the length of the samples and other details of the **corpus design** are an identical match to those of the **Brown Corpus** (hence Frown's name), but it samples from a period thirty years later. It was compiled at the University of Freiburg and is available through the **International Computer Archive of Modern and Medieval English (ICAME)**.

Freiburg–LOB Corpus of British English (FLOB) The FLOB Corpus is a 1-million-word **corpus** of written British English from the early 1990s, created by the same team that built the **Frown Corpus** at the University of Freiburg. Just as Frown is a match for the **Brown Corpus** but sampled from a period thirty years later, so FLOB is a thirty-year match for **Lancaster–Oslo/Bergen (LOB)** in terms of its sampling frame. Brown, LOB, Frown and FLOB form a 'family' of **corpora** that between them allow linguists to analyse differences between British and American English, and between the varieties of English used in different decades. All are available through the **International Computer Archive of Modern and Medieval English (ICAME)**.

French Interlanguage Database (FRIDA) Under development at the Université Catholique de Louvain, this
corpus, being built by a team headed by Sylviane
Granger, is a **learner corpus** of **L2** French. At the time of
writing the corpus is 200,000 words in size. The goal is
to build a corpus of 450,000 words. The **data** in the
corpus has been produced by intermediate-level
language learners, and each text is 100 to 1,000 words
long. The corpus is being error-tagged according to a
scheme developed at the Université Catholique de
Louvain. The **L1** backgrounds of the speakers in the
corpus vary. See http://www.fltr.ucl.ac.be/fltr/germ/etan/
cecl/Cecl-Projects/Frida/fridatext.htm.

frequency The concept of frequency underpins much of the
analytical work that is carried out within the remit of
corpus linguistics. Frequencies can be given as raw **data**,
e.g. there are 58,860 occurrences of the word *man* in the
British National Corpus (BNC); or (often more usefully)
they can be given as percentages or proportions – *man*
occurs 602.91 times per million words in the BNC –
allowing comparisons between **corpora** of different sizes
to be made.

Frequency analyses also allow comparisons to be
made between different words in a **corpus** – for example
man (602.91 per million) tends to occur more frequently
than *woman* (225.43 per million), suggesting that *man* is
the marked or 'prototype' term. On the other hand,
homosexual (8.41 per million) occurs more than *hetero-
sexual* (3.86 per million), which in this case is due to the
term *homosexual* being marked because homosexuality
has been considered problematical and non-standard by
society in the past.

Frequency analyses can also be carried out on grammatical forms, for example to ascertain which past-tense

verb forms are more common than their corresponding present- or future-tense forms or to compare different **genres** of language – for example what are the most (and least) common words in written and spoken English, or how has use of modal verbs shifted over time. In addition, **word lists,** compiled by frequency counts of each word in a corpus can be used in order to derive **keyword** lists. Frequency counts are also used in the calculation of **collocational** and **dispersion** data as well as the **type/token ratio** of a corpus. However, care must be taken when using frequency counts. Frequencies do not explain themselves: **concordance**-based analyses are therefore required in order to explain why certain words are more frequent than others. It may also be necessary to take into account the frequencies of related terms, for example *chap*, *fella*, *bloke*, *gent* etc. as well as *man*.

full text corpus A **corpus** that contains all the texts from a particular population. In practice, however, many **corpora** are made of a sample of texts from a population. (See also **sample text corpus.**)

function words A set of words sometimes referred to as *grammatical words*, consisting of pronouns, prepositions, determiners, conjunctions, auxiliary and modal verbs. Function words are sometimes removed when calculating the **lexical density** of a text. (See also **content words.**)

Fuzzy Tree Fragments (FTFs) A system for describing a set of syntactic structures in a **parsed** corpus. Fuzzy Tree Fragments are the central search mechanism of the **International Corpus of English Corpus Utility Program (ICECUP)** tool. Each FTF is a non-specific grammatical tree structure that can be matched to a range of similar

parsing trees in the **corpus**. This process is similar to the way a **regular expression** can be used to match a range of different words in a corpus. However, FTFs match syntactic structures, not words. FTFs are represented visually, as graphical trees, and can be written by the ICECUP user or extracted from corpus **data**.

G

General Architecture for Text Engineering (GATE) GATE (Cunningham, 2002) is an architecture, development environment and framework for building systems that process human language. It has been in development at the University of Sheffield since 1995, and has been used for many R&D projects, including Information Extraction in multiple languages. The system allows for the processing and annotation of **corpora**. GATE is implemented in Java and is freely available from http://gate.ac.uk as open-source free software under the GNU library licence.

genre The word 'genre' comes from the French (and originally Latin) word for 'class'. The term is used in linguistics to refer to a distinctive type of text. However, the classification taxonomy of texts into genres is not an objective procedure. It is therefore important that corpus designers provide accurate and complete descriptions of how genre categories were arrived at in the **documentation** which accompanies a **corpus**.

Common genres within a corpus may include categories such as press, religion, fiction, private letters and academic. However, genres may be categorised into sub-genres or super-genres; for example, fiction may be subclassified into mystery, science fiction, westerns, romance and humour. The genre of a text is usually indicated in the corpus **header**, allowing comparisons between genres to be made as well as letting researchers focus on an analysis of one particular genre.

GlossaNet Hosted by the Centre for Natural Language Processing of the Université Catholique de Louvain, GlossaNet was originally developed by Cédrik Fairon of the University of Paris 7. GlossaNet allows users to generate **concordances** from daily editions of over 100 newspapers. Once saved, a query lodged with GlossaNet will result in a daily concordance of the news sources chosen. Concordances generated by the system are emailed to users. The newspapers cover twelve European languages, though the news sources used may be from beyond Europe. While one must register to use the site, registration and use is free. To use GlossaNet visit http://glossa.fltr.ucl.ac.be/.

gold standard A gold standard dataset or **corpus** is one whose **annotation** has been checked and corrected. This is typically carried out in order to evaluate automatic annotation systems, for instance **part-of-speech taggers**. Different programs can be rated on how close to the gold standard their output is. (The term originally referred to an economic system where the value of gold is the standard of comparison for the value of money.)

Gothenburg Corpus A **parsed** corpus which has encoded both formal and functional properties of constituents, including some aspects of underlying structure. The **corpus** began as a subset of the **Brown Corpus**, which was manually analysed by researchers at Gothenburg University. (See also **SUSANNE Corpus**.)

grammar As a central concept in linguistics, the word 'grammar' has many uses. Some of the uses relevant to **corpus linguistics** are discussed here.

A grammar is an explanation of how a particular language, or 'language' in general, works: what forms occur and what forms do not occur in that language. A *descriptive grammar* (or *reference grammar*) catalogues the facts of a language, whereas a *theoretical grammar* uses some theory about the nature of language to explain why the language contains certain forms and not others. Both these sorts of grammar may use corpus **data** as a basis for their claims.

Generative grammar is a formal theory of syntax associated with Noam Chomsky. It supposes that knowledge of language takes the form of innate, fixed rules (*universal grammar*) that generate the syntactic structure of each sentence. This approach to linguistics is generally opposed to the use of **corpora** for theoretical reasons (see also **corpus linguistics, competence-performance**). Other theories of grammar allow a greater role for empirical data, for example *functional grammar*.

In **computational linguistics,** a set of computer instructions that allow a program to analyse or handle language in some way may also be referred to as a grammar. In some cases these are related to one or another of the formalisms used in theoretical grammar. Some of these are *hand-crafted grammars*, based on rules designed by a linguist, for example the **Constraint Grammar Parser of English (ENGCG)**. In other cases, the information is derived automatically from a **corpus**, and in this case may be a *statistical* or *probabilistic grammar* rather than consisting of absolute rules. A *finite-state grammar* is one that models language as a system that can be in one of a limited number of states at any one time; the operation of the grammar is then described by the actions that cause the system to change from one state to another.

granularity Within an **annotation** scheme 'granularity' refers to how many categories the scheme distinguishes – that is, how subtle the differences are between the categories. A fine-grained annotation scheme is extremely precise and distinguishes many different categories. A coarse-grained annotation scheme is fairly rudimentary, distinguishing only a few categories that are obviously different from one another. For example, a **part-of-speech tagset** that only distinguished the major parts-of-speech (noun, verb, adjective, adverb etc.) would be very coarse grained. But a tagset that had categories for plural animate common noun, singular animate common noun, plural inanimate proper noun and so on, would be considered extremely fine-grained. Very fine-grained tagsets are often used for languages that mark lots of morphological distinctions on **content words**; see **morphological richness**.

Gsearch A system, developed at the University of Edinburgh, UK, that makes it possible to search **corpora** using syntactic queries even though the **corpus** does not contain any syntactic annotation. The system undertakes syntactic parsing using a chart parser to achieve this effect. The system runs under a number of operating systems and is available for use, free of charge, for academic research. For further details of the system and to download it see: http://www.hcrc.ed.ac.uk/gsearch/.

Guangzhou Petroleum English Corpus (GPEC) A **specialised corpus** containing 411,612 words of petroleum English from written British and American sources in the 1980s, compiled by the Chinese Petroleum University.

Guidelines for ToBI Labelling An annotation scheme that provides a means of **marking up** the **prosodic** features of spoken English, including such features as intonation and stress. ToBI (Tones and Break Indices) are widely used both in phonetics and speech science. See http://www.ling.ohio-state.edu/research/phonetics/E_ToBI/ for guidelines to the application of the annotation scheme.

H

hapax legomenon A Greek phrase (plural *hapax legomena*, usually abbreviated to *hapax*) meaning 'once said' and is used to describe a word that occurs only once in a text or set of texts. In **corpus linguistics**, a hapax is a word that occurs only once in a particular corpus. Hapaxes are very common (see **Zipf's law**), and have important applications in **corpus-based** studies: for example, the relative **frequency** of hapaxes in a **corpus** or single text can, like the **type/token ratio**, be used to assess how varied the vocabulary is. The analysis of hapaxes can also be used in forensic linguistics, particularly in authorship attribution or cases of suspected plagiarism.

header In most **corpora**, the **corpus** texts will utilise a header of some kind. This is a set of information *about* the text (often called **metadata**). This information is usually **encoded** in a specified format and occurs at the top of the file, before the text itself – thus the name.

Metadata can also be held separately, in corpus **documentation** or a **database**. But including it in a header can be very useful, because the header is usually structured so that it can be read and processed by a computer as well as by a human being. This has several advantages. For instance, if the categorisation scheme for the corpus texts is expressed in the headers of the various texts, a corpus **tool** which can handle the **markup** will allow the user to interact with the categorisation scheme. For example, the user could restrict a concordance to just one **genre** of texts within the corpus, and the **concordancer** could carry this out by referring to the category information in the header.

The information in a header can vary greatly. It may include the language of the text (particularly if it is a **multilingual corpus**) and the type (spoken or written). The text's category in the categorisation system used for texts in the corpus would also often be included. For a written text, the title, the author, the publisher, and the date and place of publication would normally be included. For a spoken text the header information would often include details of how, when and where the recording was made; whether the conversation was scripted (such as a speech) or spontaneous (like an everyday conversation); and information about the speakers, including their name (but see **anonymisation**), sex, age, job, what dialect they speak and their relationship to other speakers in the text. There may also be data related to the process of converting the document to a corpus file. The size of the corpus file and its last-modified date are also often given. There could also be some more general information about the corpus, its purpose, and who created and distributed it.

How exactly the information in a header is set out varies very greatly between different corpus encoding formats. In **corpora** encoded in **Standard Generalised Markup Language** (SGML) or **Extensible Markup Language** (XML), the **document type definition** (DTD) specifies which tags can occur in the header, just as they specify the tags for the text itself. Usually there will be a completely different set of elements defined for use in the

header. These create a structure for the header information not dissimilar to that found in a database. For
example, the following is a basic **Corpus Encoding
Standard (CES)** header:

```
<cesHeader version="2.0">
  <fileDesc>
    <titleStmt>
      <h.title>Gulliver's Travels: an electronic sample</h.title>
    </titleStmt>
    <publicationStmt>
      <distributor>Really Big Corpus Project Team</distributor>
      <pubAddress>Linguistics Dept., Anytown University</pubAddress>
      <availability>Worldwide</availability>
      <pubDate>June 2005</pubDate>
    </publicationStmt>
    <sourceDesc>
      <biblStruct>
        <monogr>
          <h.title>Gulliver's Travels</h.title>
          <h.author>Jonathan Swift</h.author>
          <imprint>
            <pubPlace>London and Dublin</pubPlace>
            <publisher>George Faulkner </publisher>
            <pubDate>1726</pubDate>
          </imprint>
        </monogr>
      </biblStruct>
    </sourceDesc>
  </fileDesc>
</cesHeader>
```

Particularly in SGML and XML corpora, there may be a
single additional header for the corpus itself. This will
provide information such as the title of the corpus, its
size and the terms on which it is distributed.

Helsinki Corpus of English Texts: Diachronic Part A
1,572,800-word **corpus** of English covering Old, Middle
and Early Modern English. The corpus was developed at
the Department of English, University of Helsinki,

Finland by a team led by Matti Rissanen, Ossi Ihalainen and Merja Kytö (see Kytö (1991)). Texts are drawn from the period AD 750 to 1700. The Helsinki Corpus contains approximately 1.6 million words of English dating from the earliest Old English Period (before AD 850) to the end of the Early Modern English period (1710). It is divided into three main periods: Old English, Middle English and Early Modern English – and each period is subdivided into a number of 100-year subperiods (or seventy-year subperiods in some cases). The Helsinki Corpus is representative in that it covers a range of **genres**, regional varieties and sociolinguistic variables such as gender, age, education and social class. The Helsinki team have also produced 'satellite' **corpora** of early Scots and early American English. The corpus is **encoded** in **COCOA** format. For more details of the corpus see http://khnt.hit.uib.no/icame/manuals/HC/INDEX.HTM.

Helsinki Corpus of Older Scots A **corpus** of Scots texts gathered at the University of Helsinki, Finland. The corpus is composed of 830,000 words produced in the period 1450–1700, **marked up** in **COCOA** format. See http://khnt.hit.uib.no/icame/manuals/HC_OSCOT/BIBLIO.HTM for more details.

hidden Markov model A statistical tool that is used for modelling generative sequences. A Markov model calculates the most likely sequence of categories given a sentence. The model is referred to as 'hidden' because the actual categories are unknown: for any sequence of words, there are multiple possibilities in terms of the way that they could be encoded. The hidden Markov model has been used in **corpus linguistics** as a model for **probabilistic disambiguation** of corpus **annotation**, for example, to carry out automatic **part-of-speech tagging** of **corpora**. (See also **Baum–Welch algorithm, Maximum Likelihood principle, Viterbi algorithm.**)

historical corpus A corpus consisting of texts from one or more periods in the past. Such a corpus might be used to investigate the language of an earlier period in the same variety of ways that can be employed to investigate contemporary language using corpora; however, an additional application of historical corpus **data** is in studying how language changes over time. Examples of historical corpora include the **Lampeter Corpus of Early Modern English Tracts**, the **Helsinki Corpus of English Texts: Diachronic Part**, the **Newdigate Letters** corpus, and the **Representative Corpus of Historical English Registers (ARCHER)**.

While many historical **corpora** only include texts from a single time period (for example, the Newdigate Letters), one type of historical corpus (called a **diachronic corpus**) would include texts sampled from different times over a longer period of history. The Helsinki Corpus is an example of this type.

homogeneity When discussing corpus **design**, a **corpus** is said to be homogenous if the text it contains has been drawn from one source or a narrow range of sources. For instance, a corpus consisting of the novels of a single writer would be extremely homogenous. A corpus of articles drawn from different sections of a single daily newspaper over three years would be less homogenous; a corpus sampling from several different newspapers of different countries, would be less homogenous yet. The least homogeneous **corpora** are those that aim to be representative of the language in general, including a wide range of text types and possibly speech as well as writing. For example, the **Bank of English (BoE)** is not very homogenous at all.

In most cases, there will be less variation in the language of a homogenous corpus than in a hetero-genous corpus. If the researcher's goal is to study a particular, narrowly-defined variety of language, then a homogenous corpus would be useful. If the researcher is aiming to study how a given language works *as a whole*, then a general, broadly representative corpus would be more appropriate.

homograph An ambiguous word form: two **lexemes,** or two inflectional forms of a single lexeme, which have the same shape in the written language. For instance, *can* ('be able to') versus *can* ('metal container'), or *read* (as in 'I will read it') versus *read* (as in 'I have read it'). Homographs in a text or **corpus** can create problems when running a concordance search: researchers making investigations focused on the modal verb *can*, probably do not want to have to look at examples referring to metal containers. Resolving the **ambiguity** caused by homographs is one application of **part-of-speech tagging** and **semantic tagging.**

Hong Kong University Of Science And Technology (HKUST) Corpus The HKUST corpus is a 5-million-word **learner corpus** containing essays and exam papers written in English by Cantonese students. See Milton and Tong (1991).

HTMASC A **tool** that strips **corpus** texts of **HTML en-coding.** The **tool** can be run across multiple files and is as useful on documents gathered from the web as it is on corpus texts. Available free of charge from http://www.bitenbyte.com/.

Human Communication Research Centre (HCRC) Map Task Corpus Developed by a team headed by Henry Thompson at the HCRC, University of Edinburgh, UK. The Human Communication Research Centre is an interdisciplinary research centre based at the Universities of Edinburgh and Glasgow, established in 1989 with funding from the UK Economic and Social Research Council (ESRC). It has produced the 1,470,000-word **Map Task Corpus** (Anderson et al. 1991), which consists of sixteen hours of unscripted speech from 128 conversations in an experimental setting. These were made available, along with the tasks used in the project as well as sound recordings of the original conversations, via the **Linguistic Data Consortium**.

Humanities Computing Yearbook A resource, published in 1991, which gives a survey of research in a range of fields connected to computing, for instance sources of **corpora** and centres for **archives** and research. See Lancashire (1991).

human language technology (HLT) see **natural language processing**

hybrid tagger An automatic **tagger** which uses a combination of **probabilistic** and **rule-based disambiguation** in order to making tagging decisions on a text. As Garside and Smith (1997: 102) argue, hybrid taggers are effective because they offer the best of both worlds.

Hyderabad Corpus A corpus of written British English collected by H.V. George and over 200 assistants from a range of sources (novels, plays, newspapers). The Hyderabad Corpus consists of about half a million words and was collected in India. George was one of the pioneers of **corpus-based** research in the 1960s; one of his publications included a report on a verb-**frequency** count which was one of the earliest substantial studies to use corpus-based frequency **data** in **grammatical** description (George 1963).

Hypertext Markup Language (HTML) An application of **Standard Generalised Markup Language (SGML)** for **encoding** hypertext documents. Hypertext documents can contain links to other documents, creating a network of texts. HTML has become the foundation of the **World Wide Web,** although it was not originally designed for that purpose. A more recent language, **XHTML,** reproduces HTML as an **Extensible Markup Language (XML)** application; however, **HTML** is still widely used on the web and for other purposes.

Like HTML, most modern **corpus markup** schemes are based on SGML, making it possible to use HTML documents from the web as a source of texts for **corpora.** However, the complexity of the HTML codes used in many web pages means that converting an HTML document to a well-formed corpus text is rarely straightforward.

I

IBM Manuals Treebank A **skeleton-parsed corpus** of computer manuals consisting of about 800,000 words.

ICAMET A **corpus** of Middle English prose built at the Department of English, University of Innsbruck, Austria by a team led by Manfred Markus. Divided into three parts (the prose corpus, the letter corpus and the varia corpus) the corpus is available from the ICAME archive in CD-ROM. See http://nora.hd.uib.no/icame/newcd.htm.

imaginative prose Language consisting of texts (written and spoken) that generally fall under the remit of 'fiction'. This would include literature and other forms of creative writing (novels, plays, poetry, songs). See **informative prose**.

Index Thomisticus A 10.5-million-word **database** compiled by Robert Busa from 1962 to 1966 and published in 1973. It contained almost forty volumes of the works of the philosopher and scholar Saint Thomas Aquinas (1225–1274). The database is a reference for medieval Latin.

indexer A program that creates an index for a **corpus**, so that it can be used with a **concordancer** that requires pre-**indexing**.

indexing Searching through millions and millions of words in a **corpus** for a **concordance** can be time-consuming even for a very fast computer. To speed this process up, some **concordancers** (for example **WordCruncher**, **Xaira**) use an index – a special file (or files) which gives the concordancer instructions on where to find all the instances of a particular word in the corpus. When a search is then run, the program looks up the target word in the index and goes straight to the examples in the corpus, rather than checking every word in every text from beginning to end. This makes searches much faster; the drawback is that the index must be created before the concordancer can analyse the text in the corpus, which can be a lengthy process.

information extraction The process whereby a computer program is used to isolate particular information from running text documents. The information, once found, might be **marked up** in the text, or extracted and stored in a **database**. The techniques used for information extraction are often developed using **corpora**.

information retrieval The study and use of computers as a means to isolate particular information from a large amount of **data**, such as a **corpus**, a **database**, or a network of text such as the **World Wide Web**. A web search is an example of information retrieval. **Corpora** are often used in the development and testing of information retrieval techniques.

informative prose Language consisting of text (normally written) that is generally intended to provide information (rather than, say, entertainment). Informative prose could cover **genre**s such as science, arts, commerce and finance. See **imaginative prose**.

Institut für Maschinelle Sprachverarbeitung (IMS) Corpus Work Bench Developed by **IMS** at the University of Stuttgart, Germany, this is a powerful **concordance** package that allows complex queries to be run on monolingual and **parallel** corpora. The **corpus** is **markup** aware and can read texts marked in **Standard Generalised Markup Language (SGML)**. The **concordancer** is also able to handle large **corpora** (for instance 200 million words or more). The system runs on the **Unix** platform. It is not currently **Unicode** compatible, however. See Christ (1994) for more details of the concordancer. The concordancer is available as freeware; see http://www.ims.uni-stuttgart.de/projekte/CorpusWorkbench/.

Interactive Spoken Language Education (ISLE) Corpus A **corpus** of **spoken L2** English produced by learners with

German and Italian **L1** backgrounds. The corpus was developed at Leeds University, UK, by a team led by Eric Atwell and Clive Souter. The corpus contains transcriptions of the speakers' responses to a number of tasks (e.g. reading simple sentences, giving answers to multiple choice questions). The corpus is composed of 11,484 transcribed utterances and the speech recordings from which the transcriptions were made. Much of the **data** has been **annotated** to mark various pronunciation errors. The corpus is available from **ELRA**. See Atwell et al. (2003) for further details.

interlanguage A term devised by Selinker in 1972, referring to the linguistic rules and patterns that learners of a second language build for themselves. Interlanguage is usually markedly different from a person's first language and the target language. The study of interlanguage is one of the aims of building a **learner corpus**. See Selinker (1974), **second language acquisition**.

International Computer Archive of Modern and Medieval English (ICAME) An international organisation of linguists and information scientists working with English machine-readable texts. ICAME publishes a yearly journal and builds **archives** of English text **corpora** which are held at Bergen, Norway. The ICAME **corpus** collection consists of The **Brown** Family of written English corpora as well as a number of **spoken corpora** including the **London–Lund Corpus**, the **Bergen Corpus of London Teenage English (COLT) Corpus** and the **Lancaster/IBM Spoken English Corpus**. Since 1979 ICAME have held an annual conference, which usually occurs in May/June.

International Computer Archive of Modern and Medieval English (ICAME) Word Lists Four ready-made **word lists** are available for downloading from the **International Computer Archive of Modern and Medieval English (ICAME)** archive. There are word **frequency** lists for the **Freiburg–LOB Corpus of British English (FLOB)** and **Freiburg–Brown Corpus of American English (Frown) corpora,** as well as word frequency lists for the **Lancaster–Oslo/Bergen (LOB)** and **Brown corpora.** The wordlists for FLOB and Frown simply give the word frequency followed by the word in question, but the LOB and Brown wordlists give word frequency by word plus **part-of-speech tag** combination, hence the frequencies for *brown* as an adjective and as a proper noun are given separately. See http://khnt.hit.uib.no/icame/wordlist/ to download the wordlists.

International Corpus of English (ICE) The ICE project was initiated by Sidney Greenbaum in 1990 (Greenbaum, 1991). The goal of the project was to develop a series of comparable **corpora** of different Englishes. The hope was that by building corpora such as this it would be possible to compare and contrast a host of varieties of global English. In order to achieve this comparability, for each variety of English covered by the project the same sampling frame was adopted. Each corpus is constructed from 500 (300 spoken language and 200 written language) 2,000 word samples, 300 samples from spoken language and 200 from written language, to produce a 1,000,000 word corpus for each variety of English covered. At the time of writing, corpora for the following varieties of English are available via ICE: British, East African, Indian, New Zealand, Philipino and Singaporean English. Further corpora are planned, with corpora of American, Australian, Canadian, Hong

Kong, Irish, Jamaican, Malaysian, South African and Sri Lankan English under development. While the project is coordinated currently by Gerry Nelson at the Department of English Language and Literature, University College London, there are a range of teams directly involved with the construction of the corpora themselves. An good example of research output based on the ICE project is Greenbaum (1996). To find out more about the project and corpora, see http://www.ucl.ac.uk/english-usage/ice/.

International Corpus of English Corpus Utility Program (ICECUP) A **corpus** analysis **tool** developed for use with the **International Corpus of English**. It is designed for the exploitation of syntactic structures in **parsed** text, such as the ICE **corpora**. ICECUP can perform a **concordance** using a **Fuzzy Tree Fragment** (**FTF**) as its search criterion, displaying syntactic information from the corpus **parsing** in the concordance lines. ICECUP can also display the grammatical trees in the corpus graphically, rather than just as text interspersed with syntactic tags. See http://www.ucl.ac.uk/english-usage/ice-gb/icecup.htm.

International Corpus of Learner English (ICLE) A **learner corpus**, consisting of 2.5 million words of English written by learners from different European mother-tongue backgrounds. The constituent parts of ICLE include the **L1** English sub-corpus named LOCNESS, as well as a number of learner sub-**corpora**, among them Chinese, Czech, Dutch, Finnish, French, German, Japanese, Spanish, Swedish and Polish. Essays contained in ICLE are usually about 500–1,000 words in length and are on literary topics or those generating debate and argument.

They are by adult writers who are at least in their third year of English studies. See Granger et al. (2002b).

International Journal of Corpus Linguistics One of the most important journals in the field of **corpus linguistics**. It presents papers on many different applications of **corpora**, including **lexicography**, linguistic theory, and **natural language processing (NLP)**. It is published by John Benjamins.

Intonational Variation in English (IviE) Corpus A **corpus** consisting of thirty-six hours of recordings of the speech of teenagers in the UK with associated **prosodically annotated** transcriptions for part of the corpus. The corpus was built at Oxford University, UK, by a team led by Esther Grabe and Francis Nolan. Nine urban varieties of modern English spoken in the British Isles are represented in the corpus with recordings being made in Belfast, Bradford, Cambridge, Cardiff, Dublin, Leeds, Liverpool, London and Newcastle. As well as recording monolingual English speakers, the corpus builders also recorded the speech of some bilinguals. The corpus **data** is composed largely of elicited rather than spontaneous speech. See Grabe and Post (2002) for more details. The corpus is available to download at http://www.phon. ox.ac.uk/~esther/ivyweb/.

introspection Introspective judgements about language arise from the linguist's thought alone; they are not based on the observable, external facts of language. There is much disagreement on how great a role introspection and intuition should have in our study of language. Some schools of linguistic theory consider the linguist's intuitions about what is grammatical and what is not to be the primary focus of what linguistics ought to be explaining. On the other hand, some linguists (including some **corpus linguists**) reject any role for introspection at all, suggesting that work on language should be based solely on analysis of naturally occurring data. Yet another position (also held by many corpus linguists) is that introspection and intuition are valuable guides in telling us what to look for in empirical data, and how to interpret what we find – but the **data** itself is indispensable to make sure our ideas are grounded in reality. (See also **empiricism, corpus linguistics, intuitive data.**)

intuitive data Also *introspective* or *invented* **data.** Unlike **attested** or **modified** data which are based on real life examples, intuitive data are invented to illustrate a particular linguistic point (Stubbs 2001: xiv).

item A searchable term. Items can be single words, for example 'dog', but they can also consist of multi-word phrases 'the dog' or either/or constructions such as 'dog/cat' (dog or cat) 'dog*' (any word beginning with *dog*: *dogs, dogged, doggy* etc.). See **wild card.**

J

Java A computer programming language that is often used for **corpus tools.** A key feature of Java software is that it can run on many different computer systems, as long as those systems are running the Java Virtual Machine. Software written in other languages, such as the C **programming language,** can only be run on one type of system; the program must be recompiled to run on a different system.

Jiao Tong University Corpus for English in Science and Technology A **specialised corpus** containing approximately 1 million words of written English from the **genres** of science and technology organised into sub-genres including computers, metallurgy, machine building, chemical engineering etc. The **corpus** was compiled by Yang Huizhong at Jiao Tong University and was constructed in order to facilitate the lexical analysis of scientific registers of English.

Journal of Quantitative Linguistics The official journal of the International Quantitative Linguistics Association; the *Journal of Quantitative Linguistics* published by Routledge presents papers on mathematical and statistical approaches to the analysis of language. A great deal of the research published in the journal involves **corpora** in some way.

JUMAN A program which can analyse the morphology of Japanese **corpus** texts. The system is designed so that it can be extended by users. It was developed at the University of Kyoto, Japan, by a team led by Maokoto Nagao (Kurohashi and Nagao, 1998). The system is available to download for use free of charge, and to trial on-line at http://www.kc.t.u-tokyo.ac.jp/nl-resource/juman-e.html.

K

keyboarding One of the most basic (and slowest) ways of **text capture** (see **compilation**), keyboarding involves simply typing the contents of a text directly into a PC using word-processing software. Because it is non-automatic, and therefore expensive and time-consuming, keyboarding is normally only adopted in **corpus** building when no other option is available (as, for instance, when the texts cannot be scanned because the quality of the original is too poor, or if the text is written using a **character set** that the scanner does not recognise – which is still unfortunately the case for some of the world's writing systems). Additionally, spoken texts normally need to be keyboarded, particularly in cases involving accurate or detailed transcriptions of speech, although it is hoped that future generations of voice recognition software may help to quicken this procedure.

key keyword A potential issue with a **keyword** analysis is that a word may appear to be key simply because it occurs extremely frequently in a very small number of texts in a particular **corpus**. For example, if a corpus consists of 1,000 equal-sized files, and the word *ironmonger* only appears fifty-eight times in one single file called 'The history of the ironmonger', a keyword analysis may show this word to be key. In order to establish whether a word is key *and* representative of the corpus as a whole, a **dispersion** plot of the word across the corpus could be examined or a list of key keywords – words that are key in multiple texts in the corpus – could be calculated therefore allowing for the potentially skewing nature of disproportionate representation.

keyword
1. A word which appears in a text or **corpus** statistically significantly more frequently than would be expected by chance when compared to a corpus which is larger or of equal size. Usually **log-likelihood** or **chi-squared** tests are used to compare two **word lists** in order to derive keywords. Keywords can be calculated automatically using Scott's **WordSmith Tools** program. Commonly found keywords include (1) proper nouns; (2) grammatical words that are often indicators of a particular stylistic profile; (3) lexical

words that give an indication of the 'aboutness' of a text. For example, the following is a list of keywords found when comparing a small corpus of essays written by learners of English with the 1-million-word **Frown Corpus** of **L1** American English: *my, I, very, nice, good, big, holiday, dog, hobby, lovely, tenis, beatiful, voleyball*. This list reveals to us what is distinctive about the learner essays – for instance, significant spelling errors (*tenis, beatiful, voleyball*), over-reliance on a small set of simple adjectives (*nice, good, lovely, big*), the main essay topics (*dog, holiday, hobby*) and the fact that the essays are generally written as first person narratives (*I, my*). (See also **key keywords.**)

2. Any word that is considered 'focal' in a text, but not through statistical measures (see, for example, the discussion by Stubbs (1996: 166)).

3. A word which is made the subject of a **concordance** (see, for example, Kennedy 1998: 251).

key word in context (KWIC)   see **concordance**

kfNgram A freeware Windows-based **n-gram** generator. The system allows users to generate a **frequency** list of all n-grams (either character or word n-grams) present in a **corpus**. See http://miniappolis.com/KWiCFinder/ kfNgramHelp.html to download the program.

Kolhapur Corpus A **first generation corpus** which consists of approximately 1 million words of Indian English, drawn from materials after 1978. The texts are selected from fifteen categories, making it parallel to the **Brown Corpus**. It was developed by Geoffrey Leech with the financial assistance of Shivaji University and the University Grants Commission.

Korean Treebank A **treebank** of the Korean language developed at the University of Pennsylvania, USA. The **corpus** consists of military training manuals that have been **parsed** using a scheme similar to that used for the Penn English Treebank. The corpus contains 54,366 words in 5,078 sentences. See http://www.cis.upenn.edu/~xtag/koreantag/ for more details.

Kučera and Francis Word List A word list of American English, produced in printed form, based upon the **Brown Corpus**. See Kučera and Francis (1967).

KWiCFinder A web-based system (a personal internet search agent) developed by William H. Fletcher of the United States Naval Academy that allows one to conduct **concordance** searches across the **World Wide Web**. Using the web as a corpus enables users to access very large, unordered, text collections in a range of languages. The system is Windows based and requires the use of Internet Explorer. The service is available free of charge at http://www.kwicfinder.com.

$\boxed{\text{L}}$

L1 A person's first language, normally the language that they learn as an infant and are most competent at using. See **learner corpus, language teaching**.

L2 A person's second language, usually one that they will learn at school or as an adult. L2 is often influenced by **L1,** so that aspects of the L2 that are similar to L1 will be easier to learn than aspects that are different. Most people are not normally as proficient in their L2 as in their L1. See **learner corpus, language teaching**.

Lampeter Corpus of Early Modern English Tracts The Lampeter Corpus is a **diachronic corpus** of English, covering the period 1640–1740. The corpus samples texts from a range of **genres** (economy, law, miscellaneous, politics, religion and science) over this period, taking samples at time frames of roughly ten years. The corpus was constructed at the University of Chemnitz by a team led by Josef Schmied (see Schmied 1994), and has been used in the diachronic study of **variation** in English (see, for example, Claridge 1997). The corpus is around 1,100,000 words in size and is **encoded** with **TEI markup**. It is available from the **International Computer Archive of Modern and Medieval English (ICAME) Archive.**

Lancaster Corpus of Children's Project Writing (LCPW) A **corpus** of project writing undertaken by British school children (Smith et al. 1998). The corpus is made up of the written project work produced by a class of thirty-seven school children in the UK. These projects were selected and researched independently by the same children over a period of three years. The LCPW is a computerised representation of the primary data and other related material. It attempts to capture as much useful information as possible about the original projects, such as their appearance, their textual content and grammatical characteristics, along with what the children and others said about them. To access the corpus visit http://bowland-files.lancs.ac.uk/lever/index.htm.

Lancaster Corpus of Mandarin Chinese (LCMC) A 1-million-word **corpus** of Mandarin Chinese created in the early 2000s using data sampled in the early 1990s, developed at the **University Centre for Computer**

Corpus Research on Language (UCREL), that has been part-of-speech tagged and is designed as a Chinese match to the **Freiburg–LOB Corpus of British English (FLOB)**. The corpus is **encoded** in **Unicode** and **marked up** in **Extensible Markup Language (XML)**.

Lancaster/IBM Spoken English Corpus (SEC) A **corpus** of approximately 52,000 words of contemporary spoken standard British English of adults sampled between 1984 and 1987 from categories including radio news, university lectures, religious broadcasts and poetry. The material is available in orthographic, phonetic and **prosodic** transcription (including features of stress, intonation and pauses) and in two versions with **grammatical tagging**. It is part of the **International Computer Archive of Modern and Medieval English (ICAME)** collection of **corpora**. See Knowles (1993).

Lancaster–Leeds Treebank A manually **parsed** sub-sample of the **Lancaster–Oslo/Bergen (LOB) Corpus** (about 45,000 words) showing the surface **phrase structure** of each sentence. The Treebank was manually parsed and prepared by Geoffrey Sampson.

Lancaster–Oslo/Bergen (LOB) Corpus A **first generation corpus** compiled by researchers in Lancaster, Oslo and Bergen. It consists of 1 million words of British English texts from 1961 derived from fifteen text categories. It is the British counterpart to the American **Brown Corpus** and is available through the **International Computer Archive of Modern and Medieval English (ICAME)**.

Lancaster Parsed Corpus A **parsed** subset of the **Lancaster–Oslo/Bergen (LOB) Corpus** developed at Lancaster University, UK, by Geoffrey Leech, Roger

Garside and Tamas Varadi. The **corpus** has been manually **skeleton parsed**. Samples of text were **parsed** from each category of LOB, providing a corpus with a total of 11,827 parsed sentences (134,740 words). The corpus is available from the **ICAME archive**. See Leech and Garside (1991) for more details of the parsing process.

language engineering see **natural language processing**

language independent tagger A **tagger** that is not restricted to one particular language (although there are often some language restrictions, for example the tagger may only function with related writing systems). Some language-independent taggers require users to specify their own language-specific **tagset**s and also need pre-tagged sample texts in order to create rules or statistics. **TreeTagger** is an example of a language independent **part-of-speech** tagger developed at the Institute for Computational Linguistics at the University of Stuttgart.

language teaching Corpora can be used in order to aid language teaching in a range of ways. For example, **concordancing** packages can be employed in **Computer-Assisted Language Learning (CALL)** or **data-driven learning** exercises, whereby the student acts as a 'language detective', using inductive reasoning to make his or her own discoveries. Corpora can be used in order to improve curriculum design by examining which forms are more frequent (and therefore worth focusing on in more detail or earlier) and they can inform dictionary and grammar design by showing frequencies of different types of uses or revealing unexpected uses of words. Additionally, a **learner corpus** can be employed in order to build a profile of common earner errors and over- and under-uses of words and grammatical patterns.

See **lexical syllabus, pedagogic corpus,** while Hunston (2002: 170–216) and Kennedy (1998: 280–94) provide useful overviews.

learner corpus James (1992: 190) writes 'The really authentic texts for foreign language learning are not those produced by native speakers for native speakers, but those produced by learners themselves.' A learner corpus consists of language output produced by learners of a language. Most learner **corpora** consist of written essays using pre-set topics produced in language-teaching classrooms.

Learner corpora are useful in studies of **second language acquisition** as they help to build a profile of learner language, particularly in terms of error analysis or for ascertaining what words, phrases, **parts-of-speech** etc. are over- or under-used by learners, compared to native speakers. For example Gillard and Gadsby (1998) found that learners tend to overuse high-**frequency** adjectives like *nice*, *happy* and *big* whereas low-frequency adjectives like *enormous*, *massive* and *huge* occur less often when compared to native speakers. They also used the **Longman Learner Corpus** to create dictionary entries (in the *Longman Essential Activator*) containing additional help boxes for about 1,200 words that learners tended to find problematic, for instance 'don't say *peoples*, *people* is a plural noun'. For more information see Granger (1998) and Granger et al. (2002a).

Learning the Prosody of a Foreign Language (LeaP) Corpus A phonetically **annotated** corpus of largely **L2** speech produced by a team led by Ulrike Gut at the University of Bielefeld, Germany. The **corpus** contains a mix of elicited and spontaneous speech from L2 speakers of

German and English (131 speakers) and some **L1** speakers of English and German (eighteen speakers). Twelve hours of recordings are present in the corpus in total. Thirty-two L1 backgrounds are represented in the L2 section of the corpus. The L2 speakers are of a range of levels of L2 proficiency. For further details see Milde and Gut (2002). The corpus is available from Ulrike Gut (ulrike.gut@anglistik.uni-freiburg.de).

Leeds Corpus of English Dialects A **corpus** based on recordings made of elderly dialect-speakers in rural England in the 1960s. These were transcribed and **part-of-speech tagged** in the late 1990s. The corpus is published by the University of Leeds.

lemma The canonical form of a word (the correct Greek plural is *lemmata*, although some people write the plural as *lemmas* and may consider *lemmata* to be somewhat pedantic). Francis and Kučera (1982: 1) define it as a 'set of lexical forms having the same stem and belonging to the same major word class, differing only in inflection and/or spelling'. Lemmatised forms are sometimes written as small capitals, for example the verb lemma WALK consists of the words *walk*, *walked*, *walking* and *walks*. In **corpus** studies, word frequencies are sometimes calculated on lemmata rather than **types**; words can also be given a form of **annotation** known as **lemmatisation**.

lemmatisation A form of automatic **annotation** that is closely allied to the identification of **parts-of-speech** and involves the reduction of the words in a **corpus** to their respective **lexemes**. Lemmatisation allows the researcher to extract and examine all the variants of a particular lexeme without having to input all the possible variants, and to produce **frequency** and **distribution** information for the lexeme. In the following list the second column of words have been lemmatised. See Beale (1987).

He	he
studied	study
the	the
problem	problem
for	for
a	a
few	few
seconds	second
and	and
thought	think
of	of
a	a
means	means
by	by
which	which
it	it
might	may
be	be
solved	solve

LEXA A **corpus** management and analysis **tool**, developed by Hickey (1993). LEXA is MS-DOS compliant and contains a suite of sixty interrelated programs for linguistic retrieval and analysis. LEXA allows the user to perform a number of (mainly non-parametric) statistical tests and can be used on any **American Standard Code for Information Exchange (ASCII)** formatted text. It also carries out **lemmatisation** and contains a **tagger**.

lexeme The base form of a word. For example, the forms *kicks*, *kicked*, *kicks* and *kicking* would all be reduced to the lexeme *kick*. Together, these variants form the **lemma** KICK.

lexical density Lexical density is a means of calculating the proportion of lexical words in a text or **corpus**, by expressing it as a percentage (Ure 1971). Unfortunately there are several interpretations of how lexical density is calculated and what exactly it measures. For example, it is sometimes calculated by dividing the number of lexical or **content words** (nouns, adjectives, adverbs and main verbs) in the text by the total number of words (or **tokens**) and then multiplying by 100 (Stubbs 1996: 71–3.). However, it can also be calculated by dividing the number of *unique* lexical words in the text by the total number of words and then multiplying by 100 (sometimes removing the **function words** first, sometimes not). Another strategy (Coulthard 1993) is to count the number of lexical words and then divide by the number of clauses. A fourth strategy is simply to divide the number of unique words by the total number of words (making lexical density the same as the **type/token ratio**). Because of such conflicting accounts, it is good practice to state exactly which technique has been used in calculating lexical density.

Ure (1971) (using the first measure described) showed that written texts tend to have a lexical density of over 40 per cent, whereas spoken texts tend to be under 40 per cent. Spoken texts are predictable because they tend to focus on a person's immediate physical environment and therefore contain more repetitions. Written texts are less restricted and are therefore less predictable. (See also **lexical richness.**)

lexical grammar The analysis of the behaviour of particular words in terms of their grammatical context. **Corpus-**

based analysis has supported the concept of a lexical **grammar** based on the view that it is difficult to make a strict distinction between lexicon and grammar. This is because lexical items must be characterised in terms of their distributions in grammatical patterns, most patterns occur with particular classes of lexical items, and many grammatical patterns are, as with lexical items, specific and therefore must be learned. See Hunston and Francis (1999).

lexical richness Sometimes used simply to refer to **lexical density**, lexical richness can also refer to a measure calculated by counting the number of lexical words in a text that occur only once (see **hapax legomenon**). See Woolls and Coulthard (1998).

lexical syllabus A syllabus for **language teaching** suggested by Sinclair and Renouf (1988) that can be built using **frequency**-based information derived from a **corpus**. A lexical syllabus is based on the argument that it makes sense to teach the most frequent words in a language first as these words tend to have a wide variety of uses. Therefore students will acquire a flexibility of language easily while also covering the main points of **grammar** in a language without needing to memorise a large vocabulary. Sinclair and Renouf suggest that high-frequency multi-functional words like *make* and *back* are therefore worth learning early.

lexicography An application of **corpus linguistics** that has aided the accuracy of dictionary citations. One of the earliest **corpus-based** dictionary projects was the **American Heritage Intermediate (AHI) Corpus** based on a 1969 survey of US schools. It was the forerunner for later projects in the 1980s such as the *Collins Cobuild*

English Language Dictionary. **Corpus-based** approaches can help dictionary creators to discover many more meanings and uses of lexical items. For example, the second edition of the *Longman Dictionary of Contemporary English* was written without reference to **corpus** data, while the third edition did use corpus **data**. The second edition gives twenty meanings of the word *know*, whereas the third edition has over forty meanings. In the 1987 edition, the phrase *I know* is described as occurring when people suddenly have an idea. But in the 1995 edition, there are other uses of *I know*, derived from the examination of **corpora**, for example to show agreement: 'I'm tired', 'I know'. Many dictionaries are now created with the help of corpus-based analysis.

lexicon A list of words. In **corpus linguistics**, this usually refers to a list of words held on computer, sometimes with extra information about each word on the list. But one may also speak of 'the lexicon of a language'. This refers to all the words that exist in that language – which cannot ever be fully listed in practice, since new words are being created all the time.

Lexicons are an important product of corpus linguistics: a **word list** from a **corpus** can be used as the basis for dictionary creation, for instance. But lexicons are also an important resource for automated corpus analysis. **Part-of-speech-tagging** and **semantic tagging** usually depend on extensive computer lexicons containing lists of word forms and the possible tags they can have. Using a lexicon means that the tagger's less reliable 'guesswork' methods only need to be used for word forms that are not in the lexicon. These tagging lexicons may be 'handcrafted', that is, written by a linguist relying on their knowledge of the language. Alternatively, they may be 'induced' by automatically scanning a corpus for all the word-and-tag combinations that it contains.

The 'mental lexicon' is a human being's knowledge of the words in their language: their forms and pronunciation, their grammatical category, what they mean and how they are related to one another (for example by synonymy, antonymy, **collocation, colligation** and other links).

Linguistic DataBase (LDB) A **database** system developed by the **Tools for Syntactic Corpus Analysis (TOSCA)** group at Nijmegen University. It includes the **Tools for Syntactic Corpus Analysis (TOSCA) Corpus** and the **Nijmegen Corpus**. See van Halteren & van den Heuvel (1990). (See also **treebank**.)

Linguistic Data Consortium (LDC) An open consortium of universities, companies and government research laboratories, hosted at the University of Pennsylvania. It creates, collects and distributes speech and text **databases**, lexicons, and other resources for research and development purposes.

Link Grammar Parser Developed by a team at Carnegie Mellon University (Sleator and Temperley, 1991), the Link Grammar Parser is an automatic **parser** which is available free of charge for non-commercial research. See http://www.link.cs.cmu.edu/link/.

log-likelihood A test for statistical significance, similar to the **chi-squared** measure that is often used in **corpus** analysis, for example for **collocation** or **keyword** analysis. Log-likelihood is sometimes called *G-square* or *G score*. Like chi squared, log-likelihood compares the observed and expected values for two datasets. However, it uses a different formula to compute the statistic that is used to measure the difference. The following formula is used to calculate log-likelihood:

$$G^2 = 2\Sigma x_{ij}(\log_e x_{ij} - \log_e m_{ij})$$

Where x_{ij} are the data cell frequencies, m_{ij} are the model cell frequencies, $\log_e$ represents the logarithm to the base e, and the summation is carried out over all the squares in the table (Oakes 1998:42). (See also Dunning (1993).)

London–Lund Corpus (LLC) The LLC is derived from the **Survey of English Usage (SEU)** at University College London and the Survey of Spoken English (SSE) at Lund University. The LLC consists of 100 spoken texts of British speakers consisting of approximately 500,000 words. It was compiled by Jan Svartvik between 1975 and 1981 and between 1985 and 1988. It is part of the **International Computer Archive of Modern and Medieval English (ICAME)** collection of **corpora**. See Svartvik (1990a).

Longman Corpus Network A group of **databases**, including the **Longman Learners' Corpus**, the Longman Written American Corpus, the Longman Spoken American Corpus, the Spoken British Corpus and the Longman/ Lancaster Corpus.

Longman Learners' Corpus Ten million words of written text produced by students learning English as a second or foreign language. It contains material produced by students from many different language backgrounds and at a variety of levels of skill. The **corpus** was compiled from essays and exam papers written by students and has been exploited to study the types of errors that learners of English make. These results have been used by the publisher Longman to enhance their learner's dictionary. (See also **learner corpus, lexicography**.)

Louvain International Database of Spoken English Interlanguage (Lindsei) A **corpus** of elicited **L2** spoken English developed by an international team led by Sylviane Granger at the Université Catholique de Louvain. The **data** gathered in this way are available as original sound recordings and orthographic transcriptions. The aim of Lindsei is to represent as many **L1** backgrounds of L2 English speakers as possible. The first corpus to be completed was a 100,000-word corpus of L1 French speakers of L2 English. **Corpora** covering German, Greek, Italian, Japanese, Polish and Spanish L1 speakers of L2 English are now also available. For an example of research based upon Lindsei see De Cock (2000).

LT Chunk Produced by the Language Technology Group, this software takes English **part-of-speech tagged** text and indicates where the major constituents (noun phrases and verb phrases) are in the sentences in the **corpus**. While limited (for example post-modifying prepositional phrases are excluded from the noun-phrase chunks) the software is nonetheless of use as a fairly reliable means of exploring the lexical constituents of noun and verb phrases. See http://www.ltg.ed.ac.uk/ for further details.

LT POS A **part-of-speech tagger** for English available from the Language Technology Group. This tagger can be run in combination with **LT Chunk**. Available free of charge for non-commercial research. See http://www.ltg.ed. ac.uk/ for further details.

LUCY A **parsed** corpus of modern British English writing produced by a team led by Geoffrey Sampson at the University of Sussex, UK. The **corpus** is arranged into seven sections with two sections being composed of professionally authored and edited work (taken from the **British National Corpus (BNC)**), one section being composed of the writings of young adults and four sections consisting of the writing of children of different age groups (9-, 10-, 11- and 12-year olds). The corpus is 165,000 words in size. See Sampson (2003) for further details.

M

Machine-Readable Spoken English Corpus (MARSEC) A revised version of the **Lancaster/IBM Spoken English Corpus**. This version of the **corpus** contains the original recordings as well as time **alignment** information to link the transcriptions and recordings. See Roach et al. (1994).

Machinese Programmes (Connexor) A suite of annotation programs available from a Finnish company, Connexor. The team who created the software has also worked on the **English Constraint Grammar Parser**. The Connexor programs work on Danish, Dutch, English, Finnish, French, German, Italian, Norwegian, Spanish and Swedish. The available programs allow for **part-of-speech tagging**, dependency **parsing**, semantic analysis (English only) and name/term identification (English and Finnish only). See http://www.connexor.com/ for more details.

machine translation Machine translation is the study of computer programs that can translate a text automatically into another language. As such it is an important field within **computational linguistics**. Machine translation is difficult to do well. It is not possible to translate a text simply by replacing each word with the corresponding word in the other language: a human translator uses a wide range of information including grammar, semantics, pragmatics and world knowledge. Some approaches to machine translation use examples from **corpora** (including **parallel corpora**) to simulate this knowledge-base. A more easily achievable goal than fully automated translation is *machine-aided translation*, in which the program assists a translator by carrying out the 'easy' bits of the translation, but leaves the difficult decisions to the human being. (See also **alignment**.)

Mann Whitney test A **non parametric test** that is used to test for differences between the medians of two independent groups. It is sometimes known as the Wilcoxan rank sum test and is based on assigning values to observations, based on putting them in rank order. It is considered to be more robust than the t-test (which is its parametric equivalent), but also less powerful.

Map Task Corpus see the **Human Communication Research Centre**

markup A term for the special codes used to annotate a **corpus**; or, the process of adding these codes to a text. See **annotation, encoding, tagging**.

Masterpiece library A **database** of 1,338 literary texts, including the Bible, the Koran, the works of Shakespeare and US government documents.

MATE workbench A program designed to assist in the process of building and using **annotated** speech **corpora**. The program was developed by a consortium of European researchers led by Laila Dybkjær at Odense University, Denmark. See Carletta and Isard (1999) for more details.

Maximum Entropy Part-of-Speech Tagger (MXPOST) A **part-of-speech tagger** for English, available for use free of charge for academic research developed by Adwait Ratnaparkhi at the University of Pennsylvania, USA. The tagger is based on a so-called maximum entropy model. See Ratnaparkhi (1999) for more details of the maximum entropy approach to natural language analysis.

Maximum Likelihood principle In **part-of-speech taggers** based on a **hidden Markov model** the Maximum Likelihood principle is one way of selecting a tag for an ambiguously-tagged word. The tag chosen is the one that is most probable, when the probabilities of all the possible sequences of tags, as calculated using the Markov model, are added together. This approach is in contrast to the **Viterbi algorithm**, where a probable sequence of tags is selected, rather than a probable tag for each word.

Measuring Text Reuse (METER) Corpus A **corpus** in which syndicated news stories produced by the Press Association in the UK are linked to a number of versions of that news story as printed in the British press. The newspapers represented in the corpus include the *Daily Express*, the *Daily Mirror*, the *Daily Star*, *The Daily Telegraph*, the *Guardian*, the *Independent* and *The Times*. The corpus allows users to explore how a news story is taken from a news source and edited for publication. The texts in the corpus were all taken from the period July 1999 to June 2000. The corpus contains 772 texts from the Press Association and 944 newspaper stories, amounting to 535,040 words and is available from the **European Language Resources Association (ELRA)**. See Gaizauskas et al. (2001).

mega-corpora see **second generation corpora**

Memory Based Tagger (MBT) A package for creating **part-of-speech taggers** created by teams from the Universities of Antwerp and Tilburg, the Netherlands, utilising a memory-based learning approach to the task (Daelmans, 1995). See Daelmans (1996) for further details.

metadata The texts in a **corpus** are **data**, so information *about* the texts in a corpus is referred to as 'metadata' (data about data). This information may include the title, author, publisher and date of a written text, or details of the speakers in a spoken text. For a corpus it may include the purposes for which the corpus was constructed, the corpus **size** and the contact details of the distributor. The metadata for a corpus or for a text is often stored in its **header**. But it may also be stored separately to the actual text in the corpus **documentation** or in a database.

Michigan Corpus of Academic Spoken English (MICASE) Developed at the English Language Institute, University of Michigan, USA, the **corpus** is composed of academic speech sampled from a range of contexts at the University of Michigan. Some 190 hours of material were recorded and orthographically transcribed to construct the corpus. The corpus is marked up in **Standard**

Generalised Markup Language (SGML) and is currently 1.8 million words in size. The corpus is freely available for academic research. See http://www.lsa.umich.edu/eli/micase/index.htm for details of how to access the corpus.

MicroConcord An MS-DOS **concordancer** designed by Scott and Johns. The number of **concordance** lines that can be seen is limited to 1,500. Concordances can be saved as text files. MicroConcord offers a fast analysis and is relatively easy to learn how to use. See Murison-Bowie (1993).

Minipar A **parser** for English developed by Dekang Lin at the University of Alberta, Canada. The program can run on Linux and Windows platforms and is available free of charge for academic research. See http://www.cs.ualberta.ca/~lindek/minipar.htm to access the parser.

modified data Data that are based on **attested data** but have been modified in some way (for instance simplified) to exclude aspects which are extraneous (Stubbs 2001: xiv). (See also **intuitive data**.)

monitor corpus see **dynamic corpus**

MonoConc Developed by Michael Barlow of the University of Aukland, New Zealand, MonoConc is a Windows-based **concordance** program available in a basic (MonoConc) and advanced version (MonoConc Pro). MonoConc is designed for use with monolingual **corpus** material, with a sister program, **ParaConc,** being designed for use with data in a **parallel corpus**. The program is not **Unicode** compliant. See http://www.athel.com/ for details of how to purchase MonoConc.

morphological analyser A computer program that analyses the form of a word to determine its morphological structure in terms of the root and affixes, compounding etc. This can be one of the steps in automated **part-of-speech tagging**, as particular affixes often indicate particular parts of speech (for instance in the word *surrendered* the *-ed* suffix indicates a verb or adjective). Morphological analysis is also important in **lemmatisation**, since the affixes must be identified if the word is to be reduced to its base form.

morphological richness A reference to how many different inflectional forms the **lexemes** of a language have. A language like English, in which there are usually only two forms of each noun and four forms of each verb, is not very morphologically rich – although some languages, for example Chinese, are even less rich. Words in morphologically rich languages such as Arabic, Finnish or Latin have many inflectional forms for cases, tenses and other grammatical categories. A language's morphological richness may affect how texts and **corpora** in that language are processed. For example, in **part-of-speech tagging** a morphologically rich language can often be tagged with less **ambiguity** than a morphologically poor language, since a particular affix or morphological form will indicate unambiguously that the word is a noun, or a verb or an adjective. (See also **morphological analyser**.)

Morphy A freely available Windows-based **morphological analyser** and **part-of-speech tagger** for German. Morphy was developed by a team led by Manfred Wettler at the University of Paderborn, Germany. See Lezius (2000) for more details of the system. The system is available to download at http://www.lezius.de/wolfgang/morphy/.

MRC Psycholinguistic Database A machine-readable dictionary containing over 150,000 entries with up to twenty-six linguistic and psycholinguistic attributes for each (for example **frequency**, familiarity, concreteness, imageability and meaningfulness of words). This allows us to distinguish between a tangible word like *house* which can be more easily identified than an abstract word like *choice*. It was conceived by Max Coltheart in 1981 and was the basis for the **Oxford Psycholinguistic Database** created by Oxford University Press.

MULTEXT Tools The Multext project was led by Jean Véronis of the University of Provence, France. The project produced a series of tools designed to aid in the process of **multilingual corpus** building and use. The tools include support for working on a range of writing systems (Boualem et al. 1996) and aligning **parallel corpora**. While not **Unicode** compliant, the tools are still of great utility. See Ide and Véronis (1994) for more details of the Multext project.

Multiconcord A Windows-based **concordance** package designed by David Woolls. The program is designed to handle **multilingual corpora,** especially **parallel corpora**. The program can automatically **align** un-aligned parallel corpora and allows for parallel concordancing. The system is not **Unicode** compliant, however. For more details of the system see Woolls (2000).

multi-dimensional analysis A statistical, comparative approach to the analysis of different **genres** of speech and writing, advocated by Biber (1988, 1989). Biber used factor analysis to identify patterns of co-occurrence among sixty-seven linguistic features, in order to show the major dimensions on which texts could vary. The five dimensions Biber identified were (1) involved vs informational production, (2) narrative vs non-narrative discourse, (3) elaborated vs situation-dependent reference, (4) overt expression of argumentation and (5) impersonal vs non-impersonal style. This type of analysis showed that variation involved degree on a linear scale, rather than being a case of simple binaries. Biber also argued that 'genre distinctions do not adequately represent the underlying text types of English' (1989: 6). For example, in terms of dimension (1) – involved vs informational – Biber found that personal letters had more in common with face-to-face spoken conversations than they did with official written documents. Therefore the distinction between written and spoken texts is not always clear-cut.

multifeature analysis see **multidimensional analysis**

Multilingual Concordancer A Java-based basic concordancing package developed by Scott Piao at the University of Lancaster. The **concordancer** allows basic concordancing functions and incorporates some tools (for instance document similarity **cluster analysis**) not found in other **concordancers**. The concordancer supports **Unicode**. The system is free for use in academic research. See http://www.lancs.ac.uk/staff/piaosl/research/download/download.htm to download the system.

multilingual corpus A **corpus** that contains texts in more than one language. An example is the **Enabling Minority Language Engineering** (EMILLE) corpus. A **parallel corpus** is a specific type of multilingual corpus in which there is a defined relationship between the texts in the different languages (usually, the texts are direct translations of one another).

Münster Tagging Project (MTP) A project initiated at the University of Münster, Germany by Wolf Paprotté. The project developed **part-of-speech tagsets** for both English and German that were designed to be isomorphic. The tagsets were used to manually annotate **corpora** of English and German in order to produce training data for the development of an automatic **tagger**. The German tagset consists of a small (53 tags) and a large (138 tags) version. The English tagset also has a small (69 tags) and large (136 tags) version. Five-hundred-thousand words of German data and 40,000 words of English data have been **annotated** using the large tagsets. The German **data** is available from the **European Language Resources Association (ELRA)**.

mutual information A statistical measure that compares the probability of finding two items together to the probabilities of finding each item on its own. In **corpus linguistics** it is often used as a measure of the strength of a **collocation** between two words.

N

named entity recognition One of the problems investigated in the field of **information retrieval**. For a computer program to assess what a text is 'about', it is useful for it to be able to identify (and tag) the names in the text: names of people, places, companies and other organisations. Doing this involves analysing the **grammar** and semantics of the text – for instance, the identification of proper nouns may involve **part-of-speech tagging** and other **computational linguistics** techniques.

national corpus Any large **second-generation corpus** that attempts to represent a range of the language used in a particular national language community is often named after its home country and dubbed a 'national corpus'. The earliest of these was the **British National Corpus (BNC)**, but this has been followed by the **American National Corpus (ANC)**, the Czech National Corpus, the Hungarian National Corpus, the Polish National Corpus and others.

natural language processing (NLP) A common term for the set of problems addressed by **computational linguistics**: getting computers to handle some aspect of language, to carry out automatically a job that a human analyst would otherwise have to do. **Alignment, part-of-speech tagging, named entity recognition** and **machine translation** are examples of applications in NLP. Many contemporary approaches to NLP make use of **corpora**: automatic analysis of a **corpus** is used to build up the base of knowledge about language that the NLP program uses to complete its task. The corpora used in NLP are often extremely large, measured in the hundreds of millions of words, and are also often relatively **homogenous**.

neologisms A new word or an existing word (or phrase) that has been given a new meaning. Neologisms are often used for naming inventions or new ideas. **Corpus-based** approaches are particularly helpful in identifying neologisms, for example Renouf (1993), using techniques which filtered out new word forms and the new contexts in which familiar words occur, analysed a 2.5-million-word **corpus** consisting of *The Times* newspaper and found 5,374 neologisms.

Network of Early Eighteenth-Century English Texts (NEET) Developed at the University of Northern Arizona, USA, by a team led by Doug Biber, this is a 3-million-word corpus of a range of registers of eighteenth-century English. The corpus is not generally available.

Newcastle Electronic Corpus of Tyneside English (NECTE) A **corpus** of English as spoken in the north east of England, developed by a team led by Karen Corrigan at the University of Newcastle. The corpus is composed of two distinct parts – one part based upon an earlier collection of spoken data made in the late 1960s by the Tyneside Linguistic Survey and a corpus of spoken data from the same area gathered in the early 1990s. The corpus from the 1960s is based upon approximately forty-three hours of data, while the corpus from the 1990s is based on roughly eighteen hours of data. For more details of the corpus see Beale and Corrigan (2000) and http://www.ncl.ac.uk/necte/.

Newdigate Letters A **corpus** of 2,100 letters written in the period 1673–1692. Most of the letters were addressed to Sir Richard Newdigate of Arbury, Warwickshire, UK. The corpus was produced by Philip Hines and totals 1,033,000 words. It is available from the **International Computer Archive of Modern and Medieval English (ICAME)**. See Hines (1995) for further details.

n-gram A sequence of n letters from a given string after removing any spaces. For example, when n=3 the n-grams that can be generated from the phrase 'how are you' are 'how', 'owa', 'war', 'are', 'rey' and so on.

N-gram statistics package A freely available tool developed by Ted Pedersen of the University of Minnesota, USA. The program extracts significant multiword sequences from **corpus data**. The program offers a range of association tests (for example **Fisher's exact test, log-likelihood, chi square**). See Banerjee and Pedersen (2003) for more details of the program.

Nijmegen Corpus A 130,000-word **corpus** of modern spoken and written British English with a full syntactic analysis of each utterance (see **treebank**).

Nijmegen Linguistic Database see **Linguistic Database (LDB)**

non-parametric test A statistical test that makes no assumptions about the population from which the **data** are drawn, unlike parametric tests which assume that the mode, median and mean are all the same and that the data follow a **normal distribution**. Although non-parametric tests are generally less powerful than their parametric counterparts, they are considered to be more appropriate for use on **corpus** data. They are also best used when a sample size is small. Commonly used non-parametric tests include the **chi square test** and the **Mann Whitney test**.

non-standard corpus A **corpus** containing non-standard language **data**, such as the Corpus of Written British Creole, the Freiburg Corpus of English Dialects (FRED) or the **Leeds Corpus of English Dialects**. See **dialect corpus, regional corpus**.

normal distribution In statistics the normal distribution is a probability distribution where there is a particular characteristic shape to the spread of the values in the data around the mean (average) value. Many quantitative phenomena in science and statistics are normally distributed. For this reason, the normal distribution is an important part of some of the statistical techniques used in **corpus linguistics**.

Northern Ireland Transcribed Corpus of Speech (NITCS) A **corpus** of approximately 230,000 words in **size** of English spoken in Northern Ireland. The corpus was built by a team led by John Kirk of Queen's University, UK and consists of orthographically transcribed conversations with a fieldworker that occurred in the period 1973–1980. The corpus is freely available for academic research from the **Oxford Text Archive**. See Kirk (1992) for more details.

Nota Bene (nb) Discourse Annotation Tool A Windows-based discourse **annotator** developed by Giovanni Flammia at MIT, USA. The system is available for download and may be used free of charge for academic research. See http://www.sls.lcs.mit.edu/sls/publications/1998/nb.zip.

Notetab Light A Windows-based freeware program, this is an **HTML** aware text editor that may be of help to **corpus** builders needing such a tool. The program can be downloaded from http://www.notetab.com/ntl.php.

Nptool A program that can identify noun phrases in English texts. Developed by Atro Voutilainen. See Voutilainen (1993) for details of the system.

$\boxed{\text{O}}$

Ogden's Basic English Word List Developed by Charles Ogden (1930) this list purports to be a list of so-called basic English terms – a list of 850 words that Ogden claimed could allow one to express some 90 per cent of all concepts in English. Available to download on-line at numerous web sites.

on-line corpus A **corpus** that can be obtained over the internet. While many **corpora** can simply be downloaded straight from the internet onto a PC, an on-line corpus usually has a web-based search engine, allowing users to browse the corpus, specify their own restrictions on searches, carry out **concordances** or look up **collocates**. Examples of on-line corpora include the **Michigan Corpus of Academic Spoken English (MICASE)**, **BNCweb** and Cobuild*Direct*. Some on-line corpora providers charge a subscription fee for full access.

Open Language Archives Community (OLAC) An attempt to create a virtual on-line library of language resources, including **corpora**. OLAC seeks to enable major language **data** archives, groups and individuals to harmonise their **archiving** practices so that the search for language resources worldwide can be facilitated via a standard interface. The interface is currently available for use at the **Linguistic Data Consortium** website.

optical character recognition (OCR) see **scanning**

Oxford Concordance Program (OCP) A batch program that can make **word lists**, **concordances** and indices from a corpus of raw text. The OCP is available from Oxford Computing Services. See Butler (1985), Lancashire (1991) and Davidson (1992).

Oxford Psycholinguistic Database Formerly the **MRC Psycholinguistic Database**, the Oxford Psycholinguistic Database was updated in 1987 by Philip Quinlan at the University of York. It comprises 98,538 English words, giving information on a range of linguistic and psycho-linguistic criteria (for example phonetics, syllable count, familiarity, **frequency** etc.). The frequency data is taken from the **Brown** and **London–Lund corpora**.

Oxford Text Archive (OTA) The OTA consists of over 2,500 texts in more than twenty-five languages. Many of these texts have been **marked up** to **Text Encoding Initiative (TEI)** standard and can be downloaded from the internet as plain text files. The OTA is part of the Arts and Humanities Data Service (AHDS), which is funded by the Arts and Humanities Research Council (AHRC).

P

ParaConc Developed by Michael Barlow of the University of Aukland, New Zealand, ParaConc is a Windows-based **concordance** program specifically designed to facilitate working with **parallel** and **multilingual corpora**. The program can use pre-aligned corpus texts or can work interactively with a user to align unaligned **data**. The program is not **Unicode** compliant. See http://www. athel.com/ for details of how to purchase the program.

parallel corpus A parallel corpus consists of two or more **corpora** that have been sampled in the same way from different languages. The prototypical parallel corpus consists of the same documents in a number of languages, that is a set of texts and their translations. Since official documents (technical manuals, government information leaflets, parliamentary proceedings etc.) are frequently translated, these types of text are often found in parallel corpora. The **Corpus Resources and Terminology Extraction (CRATER) corpus** is an example of this type of corpus.

However, another type of parallel corpus (sometimes

called a 'comparable corpus') consists of different texts in each language: it is merely the sampling method that is the same. For instance, the **corpus** might contain 100,000 words of fiction published in a given timeframe for each language.

The applications of parallel corpora include comparing the lexis or **grammar** of different languages (see **comparative linguistics**), looking at the linguistic features of translated texts, and work on **machine translation**. For many of these purposes, an important first step in processing the parallel corpus is **alignment**.

Although the term 'parallel corpus' usually refers to corpora in different languages, corpora in different regional dialects of the same language (for example, the **Brown** and **Lancaster–Oslo/Bergen (LOB)** corpora) or in the same language variety at different times (for example, the LOB and **Freiburg–LOB Corpus of British English (FLOB)** corpora) can also be considered to be 'parallel' in a similar sense.

parser A computer program that adds **parsing** tags to a text automatically: examples include **Minipar** and the **Link Grammar Parser**.

parsing When a text is parsed, tags are added to it in order to indicate its syntactic structure. For instance, the start and end points of units such as noun phrases, verb phrases, and clauses would be indicated by parsing tags. The parse might also add information about how the syntactic units relate to one another. Examples of parsed **corpora** include the **Lancaster–Leeds Treebank**, the **Penn Treebank**, the **Gothenburg Corpus** and the **CHRISTINE Corpus**. (See also **phrase structure, treebank, skeleton parsing**.)

part-of-speech tagging (POS) A type of **annotation** or **tagging** whereby grammatical categories are assigned to words (or in some cases morphemes or phrases), usually via an automatic **tagger** although human **post-editing** may take place as a final stage. A number of POS taggers are in existence, for example, the **CLAWS** taggers, the **LT POS** tagger, **Trigrams'n'Tags**, **TAGGIT**, **Text Segmentation for Speech (TESS)**, and the **Constraint Grammar Parser of English (ENGCG)** tagger.

Patrologia Latina Database An electronic version of the first edition of Jacques-Paul Migne's *Patrologia Latina*, published between 1844 and 1855, and the four volumes of indices published between 1862 and 1865. It comprises the works of the Church Fathers from Tertullian in AD 200 to the death of Pope Innocent III in 1216. It is available as a CD-ROM and as an **on-line corpus**.

pattern see **regular expression**

pedagogic corpus A **corpus** used for **language teaching** that simply consists of all of the language to which a learner has been exposed in the classroom; for example, the texts and exercises that the teacher has used. The advantage of using a pedagogic corpus is that when a language item is met in one text, the teacher can refer back to examples from previous texts to show students how to draw conclusions from additional evidence. Also, the examples will be familiar to the students, and a **concordance**-based analysis of a pedagogic corpus will be more predictable than analyses of a general corpus. See Willis and Willis (1996).

Penn Chinese Treebank A project on-going since 1998 at the University of Pennsylvania, USA to provide a large **tree-bank**ed corpus of Mandarin Chinese. The project has, to date, produced four versions of their **corpus**, with version 4.0 being current at the time of writing. The corpus is composed of text drawn from three newswire services (Xinhua, the Information Services Department of Hong Kong Special Autonomous Region and Sinorama) in the period 1994–2001. The corpus currently consists of 404,156 words, though the project aims eventually to provide a 500,000-word corpus. Details of the corpus, including **annotation** schemes and standards are available on-line at http://www.cis.upenn. edu/%7Echinese/. The corpus is available from the **Linguistic Data Consortium**.

Penn–Helsinki Parsed Corpus of Middle English This **historical corpus** consists of over a million words of Middle English text. Its **annotation** includes **part-of-speech tagging** and **parsing**. It was developed at the University of Pennsylvania, USA, alongside another historical corpus, the Penn–Helsinki Parsed Corpus of Early Modern English.

Penn Treebank A collection of **corpora** which have been **annotated** with brackets indicating where syntactic phrases begin and end in the texts, and how the phrases are nested in the structure of the sentence. Constructed at the University of Pennsylvania, USA, it includes – among other text collections – versions of the **Brown Corpus** and the **Switchboard Corpus** annotated with Penn Treebank syntactic tags. Two versions of these tags exist: Penn Treebank I bracketing and Penn Treebank II bracketing. (See also **parsing, treebank**.)

Perl A programming language often used to create programs for text-manipulation and searching. Programs in Perl are often referred to as 'scripts'.

Personal Letters Corpus A **corpus** of personal letters written by **L2** American English speakers with a Japanese **L1** background. The corpus was gathered by Yasumasa Someya of Aoyama Gakuin University, Japan. The corpus consists of 1,037 letters amounting to 141,608 words. It can be used via a web-based **concordancer** available at http://ysomeya.hp.infoseek.co.jp/.

phrase structure An important aspect of **grammar**. When we analyse phrase structure, we identify the start and end points of major syntactic units such as sentences, noun phrases, verb phrases and so on, and identify how they are 'nested', that is which phrases are part of which other phrases. For instance, in one common approach to analysing phrase structure, the sentence *The cat sat on the mat* would be analysed as follows:

> [S [NP The cat NP] [VP sat [PP on [NP the mat NP] PP] VP] S]

> Where:
> [S Sentence S]
> [NP Noun Phrase NP]
> [VP Verb Phrase VP]
> [PP Prepositional Phrase PP]

In **parsing**, these phrase structures are marked onto a corpus text, often using some kind of bracketing, as above (although the structure can also be represented visually as a tree: see **treebank**). However, parsing does not necessarily just mean phrase structure analysis, as other syntactic analysis, such as the grammatical functions of words and phrases (for example subject, object) or dependencies between words and phrases (for example a subject noun phrase is dependent on its verb) may be **marked up** in a parsed text.

plain text A text or **corpus** that does not contain any **markup** (whether **Standard Generalised Markup Language (SGML)**, **Extensible Markup Language (XML)** or other), or any added analysis such as **part-of-speech tags** and contains only the actual words of the original document, is said to be plain text. 'Plain text' normally also implies the use of a standard character **encoding** such as **American Standard Code for Information Exchange (ASCII)** or **Unicode**. (See also **raw corpus**.)

Polytechnic of Wales (POW) corpus A **corpus** consisting of about 65,000 words of naturally-occurring language **data** spoken by 120 children aged between six and twelve years in South Wales. It has been grammatically **parsed** in terms of systematic functional **grammar** and is available through the **International Computer Archive of Modern and Medieval English (ICAME)**.

portmanteau tag A solution to the issue of problematic **disambiguation**. When **probabilistic** taggers are unable to select a single **tag** for a word or phrase they may sometimes use a portmanteau tag, indicating that a firm decision could not be made but that the correct tag is likely to be one of a range of two (or more) possible outcomes. Portmanteau tags are often indicated by using a hyphen, for instance within the CLAWS C5 tag set, used to tag the **British National Corpus (BNC)**, the tag NN1-AJ0 is a portmanteau tag consisting of 'singular common noun or adjective'. In general, the more likely possibility is given as the first half of the pair.

post-editing Most automatic **taggers** tend not to be 100 per cent **accurate**, for example, Smith (1997) notes a 3–5 per cent error rate for the automatic **part-of-speech tagging** of English texts. In order to improve accuracy towards

100 per cent, human editors are sometimes employed to correct **tagging errors** by hand. Such measures often improve accuracy, for example Baker (1997) found a mean accuracy of 99.11 per cent between four human post-editors (an improvement of 1.9 per cent compared to the computer tagger). However, as well as accuracy of post-editors, **consistency** (both inter-rater and intra-rater) also needs to be taken into account, particularly in cases where a word's part-of-speech is potentially ambiguous. Factors such as the prior experience of post-editors, amount of training given, the amount of communication between different post-editors and the size and complexity of the **tagset** are all likely to have an impact on overall accuracy and consistency.

postmodification A study of postmodification by de Haan (1989), using the **Nijmegen Corpus,** found that almost 98 per cent of postmodifying clauses had simpler clause patterns, compared to 92 per cent of non-postmodifying clauses. Biber et al. (1994) used part of the **Lancaster–Oslo/Bergen (LOB),** corpus, finding that post-nominal modification by prepositional phrases is more frequent than full, finite relative clauses.

post-processing The process of running a text that has been manipulated by a computational **tool** through an additional program. Typically, a post-process would affect the **encoding** format of the text, and might be applied to the text output by an **annotation** tool such as a **part-of-speech tagger**. It is common for taggers and similar programs to output text in a specific, non-standard format. Post-processing is then needed to convert the tagged text to **Standard Generalised Markup Language (SGML), XML** or another standardised format for use in **concordancers**. Post-processing is an entirely automatic process that does not affect the actual tags; as such, it should not be confused with **post-editing**.

Prague Dependency Treebank A **parsed** corpus of Czech, consisting of texts drawn from the Czech National Corpus with part-of-speech and syntactic **annotation**. See http://ufal.ms.mff.cuni.cz/pdt.

precision and recall Precision and recall are a pair of measures, taken from the field of **information retrieval**, that can be used to measure how successful an automated **tagger** is. The performance of a tagger that only assigns one tag to each token can be measured with just a single score, **accuracy** or 'correctness', which is the percentage of tokens that have the correct tag. But many taggers can assign more than one tag to each token, so a single measure of correctness will not suffice: precision and recall are often used instead.

Recall measures, roughly speaking, how many correct tags have been assigned by the tagger. It is equal to the number of tokens tagged correctly divided by the total number of tokens tagged. *Precision* measures how many unwanted tags the tagger has removed from the text. It is equal to the number of tags correctly assigned in the text, divided by the total number of tags assigned. Both precision and recall are expressed as percentages, with scores closer to 100 being better in both cases (see also van Halteren (1999)),

In information retrieval, recall measures how much of the desired information has been retrieved, and precision measures how much undesired information has been retrieved along with it.

pre-electronic corpus **Corpus-based** research that occurred before the 1960s is generally categorised as pre-electronic and consisted of work in five main areas: biblical and literary studies, **lexicography**, dialect studies, language education studies and grammatical studies (Kennedy 1998: 13). Such research was often painstakingly carried out, using index cards and human labour to calculate **frequencies** by counting. See, for example, Thorndike and Lorge's frequency lists (1944) and Fries' studies of grammar (1940, 1952). (See also **corpus linguistics**.)

probabilistic disambiguation A set of methods for choosing the correct tag in automatic corpus **annotation** that rely on **probability** or statistics to make a good guess at what the correct tag is likely to be. These statistics are **frequencies**, and are often derived from previously annotated **corpora** in order to perform a subsequent analysis on untagged texts. See Garside et al. (1987). (See also **hidden Markov model, rule-based disambiguation**.)

probability A goal of **corpus linguistics** is to account for language in terms of whether something is possible and/or probable (Kennedy 1998: 270). Using **frequency** data derived from **corpora**, coupled with statistical tests, we can go beyond measures of whether a particular linguistic feature is possible, but say the extent to which it is probable in actual language use. Probability therefore allows for a more gradated account of language use.

problem-oriented tagging The phenomenon (as described by de Haan (1984)) whereby users will take a **corpus**, either already **annotated** or unannotated, and add to it their own form of annotation, oriented particularly towards their own research goal. It is not an exhaustive process, so not every word or sentence needs to be tagged, only those which are directly relevant to the research questions being asked. In addition, annotation schemes are selected with these research questions in mind.

proclitic A proclitic is a **clitic** which attaches to the beginning of the following word. See **enclitic**.

Project Gutenberg A massive internet **archive** of over 16,000 copyright-free books stored as machine-readable text. It is accessible at http://www.gutenberg.org. Additional texts are continually being added to the collection; books are distributed as **plain text**.

proofreading One of the final processes of **text capture** involving **corpus** building, particularly when texts have been **keyboarded** or electronically scanned. An automatic spell-check is rarely 100 per cent accurate at targeting errors, so additional human checking is required.

PROSICE Corpus This corpus consists of a set of spoken texts from the British section of the **International Corpus of English** (**ICE**) with time-**alignment** and syntactic **annotation**. It was created for the study of English **prosody**.

prosody
1. Prosodic features of spoken language (such as speed, volume and pitch) can be **annotated** in a **corpus**, allowing for a more sophisticated analysis.
2. Prosody also refers to patterns in language that are revealed via corpus analysis (often via looking at **concordances** or **collocations**). See **semantic prosody**, **discourse prosody**, **semantic pattern**.

punctuation marks Along with **accented characters**, punctuation marks can sometimes be rendered differently on different platforms, particularly those that occur outside the **American Standard Code for Information Exchange (ASCII)**. It is therefore suggested that **corpus** builders represent punctuation marks as entities, delimited by the & and ; characters. Table 7 gives examples of the standard entity references for punctuation.

Table 7. Some standard entity references for punctuation

entity reference	punctuation	punctuation mark
&ldquo;	left double quotation mark	"
&rdquo;	right double quotation mark	"
&mdash;	one-em dash	-
&hellip;	horizontal ellipsis	…
&rsquo;	right single quote	'
&lsquo;	left single quote	'
&lsqb;	left square bracket	[
&rsqb;	right square bracket	]
&verbar;	vertical bar	|
&lcub;	left curly bracket	{
&rcub;	right curly bracket	}

rank ordering

1. A common way of presenting **frequency** information in **word lists** is to present them in rank order, for example the most frequent word is given first. This is opposed to, say, presenting the list alphabetically.
2. A technique used in some **non-parametric** statistical tests, for instance the Wilcoxon test or the **Mann-**

Whitney test, that involves carrying out the test using ranked values of raw frequency data, rather than using actual frequencies.

raw corpus A corpus that has not been processed in any way. Particularly, it is a corpus to which no analytic annotation (such as parsing) has been applied. (See also plain text.)

Reading Academic Text Corpus A corpus constructed to study the use of English in an academic context; it consists of research articles and Ph.D. theses written by staff and students at Reading University. See http://www.rdg.ac.uk/AcaDepts/cl/slals/corpus.htm.

Reading/Leeds Emotion in Speech Corpus A spoken corpus constructed with the aim of investigating how properties of speech such as intonation relate to the emotions that human beings perceive as being expressed in speech. As such its text is annotated for intonation and for emotional content. See http://www.rdg.ac.uk/AcaDepts/ll/speechlab/emotion/.

recall see precision and recall

reference corpus When using frequency-based techniques to analyse a text or set of texts, it is necessary to have something with which to compare them. This is necessary, for instance, if we wish to establish that some word or form is more common in a particular text than is normally expected. The basis for the comparison is often a larger set of texts drawn from a wider range of genres and/or sources. This larger dataset is often called a reference corpus.

Typically, for English, a reference corpus would be

one from the **Brown** family of **corpora** or one or more
sections of the **British National Corpus (BNC)**. The term
'reference corpus' may also be used to describe any
corpus that, like these corpora, is not a sample of any
particular language variety, domain or text type, but is
instead an attempt to represent the general nature of the
language through a wide-sampling corpus **design**.

regional corpus A **corpus** consisting of language from a
particular region, which is often compiled in order to
investigate regional or sociolinguistic variation. (See also
dialect corpus, non-standard corpus.)

regular expression A type of **string** that may include special
characters (sometimes called '**wild cards**') that mean the
regular expression as a whole will match with more than
one string. For instance, the full stop . as a special character in a regular expression can represent any single
letter. If so, the regular expression *b.d* would match with
the strings *bad*, *bbd*, *bcd*, *bdd*, *bed* etc. Regular expressions, sometimes known as *patterns*, are often used
when searching a **corpus**. It is often easier to define a
regular expression that matches the set of words in a
search, than to search for each word individually and
combine the results. For example, for an investigation
into compound words of which the second element is
-house (for instance, *greenhouse, hothouse*) a search
could be made for *.*house*. The precise rules of what the
special characters in regular expressions are and how
they work may vary in different **tools**.

relational database A **database** that stores **data** in a number
of separate data tables, that are linked by means of *keys*
that identify particular records. A record in table A can
be linked to a record in table B if one of the fields (or

columns) in table A contains the key of the record in table B. In **corpus linguistics**, relational databases are sometimes used to store **corpora**, as an alternative to storing them as **marked-up** text files.

For example, one table might contain the words in the **corpus**, with each record containing a single word, together with other fields to indicate where that word occurs in the corpus, what **part-of-speech** tag it has and so on. These fields would link the record to other tables; for example, the part-of-speech tag might link to a table listing all the part-of-speech tags and containing information about the category that the part-of-speech tag indicates. Storing a corpus in a relational database allows the corpus to be searched using database queries, rather than requiring software designed specifically for corpus analysis.

Representative Corpus of Historical English Registers (ARCHER) Corpus A **corpus** covering ten registers of English, both British and North American, over a period of 340 years (1650–1990). The corpus contains 1,037 texts, amounting to 1.7 million words. It covers both written (letters for example) and so-called speech-based (for instance drama) **genres**. The corpus is not generally available and is held at the University of Arizona. See Biber et al. (1994) for a fuller description.

representativeness One of the key claims it should be possible to make of a **corpus** is that it is a representative sample of a particular language variety. There are many safeguards that may be applied in sampling to ensure maximum representativeness in corpus **design**. Random sampling techniques are standard to many areas of science and social science, and these same techniques are also used in corpus building. Biber (1993) emphasises that the limits of the population that is being studied must be defined as clearly as possible before sampling procedures are designed. One way to do this is to use a comprehensive bibliographical index – this was the approach taken by the **Lancaster–Oslo/Bergen (LOB) Corpus** builders who used the *British National Bibliography* and *Willing's Press Guide* as their indices. Another approach could be to define the sampling frame as being all the books and periodicals in a particular library that refer to a particular area of interest. This approach is one that was used in building the **Brown Corpus**. Biber also points out the advantage of determining beforehand the hierarchical structure (or strata) of the population. This refers to defining the different **genres** or channels etc. of which it is composed. Stratificational sampling is never less representative than pure probablistic sampling, and is often more representative, as it allows each individual stratum to be subjected to probablistic sampling. However, these strata (like corpus **annotation**) are an act of interpretation on the part of the corpus builder and others may argue that genres are not naturally inherent within a language. See **sample text corpus, validity.**

robust A robust program or method is one that does not stop working, or produce nonsense results, if applied to poorly formed input. In **computational linguistics**, a robust **tool** is one that can deal at least in part with the 'messiness' of actual language in use. This messiness includes things such as sentence fragments, grammatical errors, lists, acronyms, formulas, plus (in spoken data) slips of the tongue, false starts, hesitations, filler noises and so on. So, for instance, a robust **part-of-speech tagger** or **parser** could be used on text containing these messy elements, and the messy elements would still be analysed and tagged/parsed. In general, robustness is a desirable trait for corpus analysis tools.

rule-based disambiguation A technique in **tagging** that uses rules rather than probabilities to determine which is the correct tag for a given linguistic item in a **corpus**. For example, if a word that might be a noun or a verb is preceded by an adjective and followed by a verb, then it should be tagged as a noun.

S

Saarbrücken Corpus of Spoken English (ScoSE) A **spoken corpus** of North American English, consisting of transcriptions of conversations, interviews, stories and jokes. See http://www.uni-saarland.de/fak4/norrick/scose.htm.

sample corpus Many **corpora** are not freely available to all, either because the texts in the **corpus** are subject to copyright restrictions, or because the corpus builders need to recoup the costs of creating the corpus by charging researchers for access to it. Often, in this case, a subset of the texts in the corpus will be released for free or at a very low price: this is usually called a *sample corpus*. Many of the large **second generation corpora** such as the **British National Corpus (BNC)** have associated sample corpora (see **British National Corpus sampler**), usually making up somewhere between 1 per cent and 10 per cent of the entire corpus.

A small section of a corpus that has been constructed or annotated for demonstration purposes, before the full corpus exists or has been annotated, may also be referred to as a sample corpus.

sample text corpus A corpus that is designed in order to be representative of a particular language variety (not necessarily language as a whole). It may consist of complete texts or samples taken from parts of texts. In general, the more specialised the language variety, the smaller the sample needs to be. However, Kennedy (1998: 21) warns that some **corpora** are not suitable for certain types of research: samples of texts may not be appropriate for carrying out stylistic or discourse studies, where we would expect to find different types of linguistic features at different points in a text.

scanning An increasingly popular technique of **text capture** when the original text only exists in paper form. Scanning involves the use of a scanner (which resembles a small photocopier or fax machine) and optical character recognition (OCR) software which converts the text on paper to electronic form. Scanning is not 100 per cent error-free and factors such as typeface used, presence of tables, footnotes and layout of text as well as the colour and quality of the paper can all have an impact on accuracy.

second generation corpora A term referring to **corpora** created during or after the 1990s. Such corpora are sometimes referred to as **mega-corpora** because of their large size (for example 100 million words or more). Examples of second generation corpora include the **British National Corpus (BNC)**, the **Bank of English (BoE)** and the **Longman Corpus Network**. (See also **first generation corpus**.)

second language acquisition A popular application of **corpus linguistics** is in studies of second language acquisition, and a number of **corpora** have been assembled for this purpose. These include **learner corpora** such as the **Longman Learner Corpus** or the **International Corpus of Learner's English** which are designed to reveal profiles of learner language or **interlanguage**. Native speaker/writer corpora, such as the **British National Corpus (BNC)** can also be used in order to help learners to obtain a better understanding of the norms of the target language as well as the contexts in which certain words or phrases are best used. For example, Johns (1997) outlines **data-driven learning**, which involves learners carrying out **concordances** in order to explore naturally-occurring language phenomena. Additionally, a **pedagogic corpus** (Willis & Willis 1996), consisting of all the language that a learner has been exposed to in the classroom (texts and exercises) can be used so that teachers can refer back to examples from previous texts when a new language item is encountered. The examples are likely to be familiar to students, so the concordances will be more predictable than when looking at a general **corpus**. Other types of **corpus-based** studies can aid curriculum design, for instance Mindt's (1996) comparison of the use of modal verbs in German text books for teaching English with a corpus of spoken English: he found that native speakers commonly tend to use 'will' when they want to talk about future time reference. However, in German text-books, 'will' tended to be introduced to the students about halfway through the second year, whereas less frequent modal verbs were covered much earlier by the textbooks. (See also **language teaching**.)

segmentation The process of splitting up running text into smaller units such as sentences or words (or even morphemes). Segmentation is usually done automatically by specially designed software.

Splitting a text into words, which is usually called

tokenisation, is commonly referred to as segmentation if the writing system of the language in question does not use spaces between words (for instance, Chinese). For languages such as this, word segmentation is not a trivial task.

semantic preference A term similar to Louw's (1993) concept of **semantic prosody**. Semantic preference is, according to Stubbs (2001: 65), 'the relation, not between individual words, but between a lemma or word-form and a set of semantically related words'. For example, in the **British National Corpus (BNC)** the word *rising* tends to co-occur with words relating to work and money: *incomes*, *prices*, *wages*, *earnings*, *unemployment* etc. Semantic preference also occurs with phrases. For example, the phrase *glass of* co-occurs with a lexical set of words that could be categorised as 'drinks': e.g. *sherry*, *lemonade*, *water*, *champagne*, *milk* etc. Semantic preference is therefore related to the concepts of **collocation** and **colligation**, but focuses on a lexical set of semantic categories rather than a single word or a related set of grammatical words.

Semantic preference is related to the concept of **discourse prosody**, although the difference between the two is not always clear-cut. Stubbs (2001: 65) says it is partly a question of how open-ended the list of collocates is. So it may be possible to list all of the words for 'drinks', indicating a semantic preference, but a more open-ended category such as 'unpleasant things' might be seen as a discourse prosody. Stubbs (2001: 88) later notes that even a category of semantic preference will be open-ended, but will contain frequent and typical members.

In addition, semantic preference denotes aspects of meaning that are independent of speakers, whereas discourse prosody focuses on the relationship of a word to speakers and hearers, and is therefore concerned with attitudes. Semantic preference is therefore more likely to occur in cases where attitudes are not expressed.

semantic prosody A term popularised by Louw (1993) and also used by Sinclair (1996), referring to the idea that words **collocate** in language use with specific semantic groups as well as with individual words. For example, the word *hair* may collocate with semantic groups such as length (*long*, *short*) and colour (*red*, *blonde*, *black*). Examination of **concordances** generally helps to reveal the existence of semantic prosodies. The concept is also referred to as a *semantic pattern* or **semantic preference** by others, for instance Stubbs (2001). (See also **discourse prosody**.)

semantic tagger A piece of software that attaches codes to words based upon their semantic function. An example of a semantic tagger would be the **UCREL Semantic Analysis System (USAS)** (Wilson and Thomas 1997).

SGML-Aware Retrieval Application (SARA) A software package designed specifically for use with the **British National Corpus (BNC)**. It enables users to search rapidly through the BNC, displaying **frequencies** and **concordances** of specific words, phrases, patterns of words etc. It is compatible with **Standard Generalised Markup Language (SGML)** and aware of the **annotations** in the BNC, allowing searches to be performed on combinations of words and grammatical tags. Searches can be limited to particular SGML contexts (for example, within a particular kind of element such as the title of a book or a spoken utterance), or to particular kinds of text (such as newspaper texts only or the speech of young men). See Burnard (1995), Aston and Burnard (1998).

size One of the most common questions concerning **corpus** building is 'how large should a corpus be?' In addition to the size of the corpus, the sizes of samples of texts within a corpus also need to be considered. Ultimately, size depends on a number of factors. For example, how restricted is the **genre** of language to be gathered? Shalom's (1997) study of personal adverts used a corpus of only 766 adverts (about 20,000 words), whereas the **British National Corpus (BNC)**, which contains written and spoken language from a variety of genres and time periods, contains 100 million words. However, smaller **corpora** (for instance those of one million words) that are typical of one variety of language, for example British English, Indian English, collected in a relatively short time period, are still viewed as adequate for comparative work (Leech's (2002) study of modal verbs across the **Brown** family of corpora, for example). Additionally, what is the purpose of building the corpus? for **collocations** or to derive word meanings from **concordances**, say. Kennedy (1998: 68) suggests that for the study of **prosody** 100,000 words of spontaneous speech is adequate, whereas an analysis of verb-form morphology would require half a million words. For **lexicography**, a million words is unlikely to be large enough, as up to half the words will only occur once (and many of these may be polysemous). However, Biber (1993) suggests that a million words would be enough for grammatical studies. Finally, **corpus-based** analyses do not always need to be carried out on corpora: Stubbs (1996: 81–100) carried out a comparative corpus-based analysis on two speeches by Baden-Powell, consisting of under 1,000 words of **data** in total. Although this was a small amount of data, he was still able to indicate significant differences in usage between the two speeches, based on concordances and collocations of various key lexis.

skeleton parsing A set of procedures for simplified **parsing** of sentences, developed by Leech and Garside (1991). Skeleton parsing is carried out manually, using software to speed up **data** entry.

specialised corpus A **corpus** which has been designed for a particular research project, for example, **lexicography** for dictionary **compilation,** or to study particular specialist **genres** of language: child language, English for Academic Purposes etc. (See also **learner corpus, dialect corpus, non-standard corpus** and **regional corpus.**)

Speech Act Annotated Corpus for Dialogue Systems (SPAAC) This **spoken corpus** contains **annotations** particular to spoken text: the **corpus** is **marked up** in **Extensible Markup Language (XML)** format for the speech acts of the individual utterances within the corpus, which were applied partly manually and partly automatically.

Speech Analysis Tools A software suite that provides the ability to view and to add **annotation** to speech waveforms. Available for free from http://www.sil.org/computing/catalog/show_software.asp?id=59.

speech corpus This term is sometimes used to refer to a specialised form of **corpus,** not to be confused with a **spoken corpus.** A speech corpus consists not of transcriptions, but of recordings, usually made in a studio, that are used to study pronunciation and other aspects of phonetics and phonology in depth. In some cases, a speech corpus may not consist of natural data – the participants may be reading out words or sentences set by the researcher. An example is the **TIMIT Corpus**.

Speech, Thought and Writing Presentation Corpus A **corpus** developed at Lancaster University to investigate the different ways in which reported language is presented in texts, an important issue in stylistics. The corpus is **annotated** to indicate different types of presentation, for instance, direct reported language versus indirect reported language. See http://www.ling.lancs.ac.uk/stwp.

spoken corpus A **corpus** consisting entirely of transcribed speech. This could be from a range of sources: spontaneous informal conversations, radio phone-ins, meetings, debates, classroom situations etc. Spoken **corpora** can present problems to traditional **taggers** due to repetitions, false starts, hesitations, vocalisations and interruptions that occur in spontaneous speech. Compared to **written corpora,** spoken corpora tend to have a higher proportion of pronouns (particularly first and second person) and discourse markers. However, Biber (1998) has shown that some spoken and written **genres** are remarkably similar to each other (for example personal letters and face-to-face conversations) in terms of frequencies of certain linguistic phenomena.

SRI American Express travel agent dialogue corpus This is a large **spoken corpus** made up of transcribed telephone conversations between travel agents and customers. The corpus texts are on-line at http://www.ai.sri.com/~communic/amex/amex.html.

Standard Generalised Markup Language (SGML) A standard way, created in the 1980s, of encoding electronic texts by using tags (developed from a system known as **COCOA references**) to define typeface, page layout etc. In general, the codes are enclosed between less than and greater than symbols: < >. These codes are often referred to as 'elements'. So for example the code <p> is used to indicate the start of a new paragraph. However, many codes also have a corresponding closing or end tag, which is demonstrated by the use of a forward slash / sign after the less than symbol. So the end of a paragraph would be encoded as </p>.

Elements may also contain what are called 'attributes'. For example, the code <pause dur=4> could be used in a spoken transcription to indicate the occurrence of a pause during speech, the duration being 4 seconds. Here, the attribute is *dur* (duration) and its value is 4 (seconds).

Different forms of SGML have been employed for a range of purposes. So **HTML** (Hyper Text Markup Language) uses a predefined set of codes based around the general SGML rules. For example, bold print is specified in HTML with the code pair <b> and </b>. See Bryan (1988) and Goldfarb (1990) for more information about SGML. (See also **Text Encoding Initiative (TEI)**.)

standardisation When comparing frequencies across or within **corpora**, it is often useful to standardise the results in order to take into account the fact that files or corpora may be of different sizes. This can be achieved by expressing frequencies as a percentage or as occurrences per *x* words. Table 8 shows frequencies for the six age groupings in the **British National Corpus (BNC)** for the word *cheerio*.

Table 8. Frequencies for *cheerio* in six age groupings

Age category	Total number of words spoken in category	Frequency of cheerio	Frequency of cheerio per million words
0–14	383,233	2	5.22
15–24	590,264	8	13.55
25–34	1,111,255	9	8.1
35–44	1,067,047	12	11.25
45–59	1,624,720	27	16.62
60+	1,129,298	66	58.44
Total	5,905,817	124	21

Although the word *cheerio* appears more often in the 35–44 age range than the 15–24 range, because the 35–44 section of the corpus is almost twice as large as the 15–24 section, the word occurs proportionally more often in the 15–24 age range.

standardised type/token ratio One problem when calculating the **type/token ratio** in a **corpus** is that the larger the corpus, the lower the type/token ratio is likely to be. This is because high **frequency** words like *the* tend to be repeated whereas the probability of new types of words appearing will always decrease, the larger the corpus size. Therefore, the type/token ratio tends to reveal more about corpus size than lexical repetition or uniqueness.

For example, the **Freiburg–LOB Corpus of British English (FLOB)** Corpus is made up of fifteen files of different sizes. From Table 9, it can be seen that the larger the file, the smaller the type/token ratio tends to be.

Table 9. Type Token Ratios of the 15 texts

File name	Size (words)	Type token ratio
M	12,208	28.20
R	18,313	24.97
D	34,618	17.12
C	34,744	23.90
L	48,466	13.77
B	55,001	16.05
P	58,627	12.71
K	58,759	14.23
N	58,846	14.73
H	61,597	10.92
E	77,717	15.16
F	89,864	13.25
A	90,204	13.50
G	156,909	11.26
J	164,714	9.16
Total FLOB	1,020,623	4.56

A solution to the skewing effect of corpus size is to calculate a standardised type/token ratio (sometimes referred to as the 'mean type/token ratio'). This is achieved by obtaining the type/token ratio for, say, the first 2,000 words in the corpus (or however many words are specified), then the next 2,000 words, then the next and so on. The standardised type/token ratio is calculated by working out the average of all of these separate type/token ratios, providing a more representative figure. Using this technique, the standardised type/token ratio of FLOB therefore works out at 46.03.

static corpus A **sample text corpus** that is intended to be of a particular **size** – once that target is reached, no more texts are included in it. Most **corpora** are static, providing a 'snapshot' of a particular language variety at a given time. (See also **dynamic corpus, monitor corpus.**)

stem The part of a word to which inflectional affixes are added; conversely, it is the part that remains when affixes are removed. For instance, *walk* is the stem of *walks*, *walked* and *walking*. Isolating the stem of a word is important for **lemmatisation**, and is often done by a **morphological analyser**. (See also **lemma.**)

stochastic tagging see **probabilistic disambiguation**

string A sequence of letters, numbers or other symbols, usually relatively short. The term comes from computer science; on a computer, each symbol is encoded as a number (referred to as a 'character') and an adjacent set of characters in a computer's memory is called a 'string'. The term 'search string' refers to a string that a program looks for as it goes through a text or **corpus**, for example when creating a **concordance**.

Surface and Underlying Structural Analyses of Naturalistic English (SUSANNE) Corpus A **corpus** created with the purpose of developing a taxonomy and **annotation** scheme for the grammar of English for **natural language processing**. It consists of about 128,000 words of the **Brown Corpus** annotated using the SUSANNE scheme, each word being tagged via six fields covering (1) reference and (2) status (both of which show whether the word is an abbreviation or symbol), (3) word-tag (showing part-of-speech category), (4) the word itself, (5) its **lemma** and (6) how it is parsed in the context of the sentence it appears in. See Sampson (1995).

Survey of English Usage (SEU) Corpus Founded in 1959 by Randolph Quirk in order to provide an account of spoken and written British English, with both genres being represented about equally. It contained 200 text samples of about 5,000 words each, collected between 1953 and 1987. It was a **pre-electronic corpus**, consisting of a paper slip for each word **token** in the corpus. Each slip contained seventeen lines of text and was marked as a case of one of sixty-five possible grammatical features and 400 function words or phrases. It provided the basis for a complete description of English grammar (see Quirk et al. 1985). The spoken section was eventually published in electronic form as the **London–Lund Corpus**.

Switchboard Corpus A large American English **spoken corpus**. It consists of transcribed recordings of telephone conversations from the early 1990s. It is around 3 million words in size, and is made up of over 2,000 conversations lasting more than 240 hours. See http://www.cavs.msstate.edu/hse/ies/projects/switchboard/index.html.

synchronic corpus A **corpus** in which all of the texts have been collected from roughly the same time period, allowing a 'snapshot' of language use at a particular point in time. (See also **diachronic corpus**.)

T

tagger Software which automatically carries out **tagging** on a corpus. See also **annotation, post-editing, hybrid tagger, part-of-speech tagging, semantic tagger, template tagger, training corpus**.

tagging A more informal term for the act of applying additional levels of **annotation** to corpus **data**. A tag usually consists of a code, which can be attached to a phoneme, morpheme, word, phrase or longer stretch of text in a number of ways, for example, using **Standard Generalised Markup Language (SGML)** elements, or by using an underscore character between a word and its tag (for example cat_NN1 is the word *cat* tagged as a singular common noun using the **CLAWS** C7 **tagset**). Tagging is often carried out automatically using software (see **tagger**). However, human **post-editing** is also often required as a final stage. (See also **ditto tags, part-of-speech tags, portmanteau tag, problem-oriented tagging, stochastic tagging, tagging errors, tagset, tag stripping**.)

tagging errors Automatic **taggers** are not usually 100 per cent accurate, hence the need for human **post-editing**. In general, texts that contain rare words (which are likely to be unfamiliar to the **tagger**), foreign words (which may not work well with the tagger's morphological rules), specific **genres** that use language in an unpredictable, playful or creative way (for instance jokes, poems) or genres which do not conform to standard grammatical rules (for example informal spoken conversations) are likely to contain higher numbers of tagging errors than texts that are more predictable and typical of a standard language variety. The application of **portmanteau tags** is one way in which errors can be minimised. (See also **robust**.)

TAGGIT An early **part-of-speech tagger** developed by Greene and Rubin (1971) that was used to tag the **Brown Corpus**. Its **tagset** contained eighty-seven tags, including major word classes and their inflectional variants, function words and other important lexemes such as *not*. It assigned the correct tag 77 per cent of the time to the Brown Corpus and despite its relatively low accuracy rate, provided a basis for more advanced taggers that were to follow.

tagset A collection of tags (or codes) that occur in an **encoding** or **tagging** scheme used to **annotate corpora** in order to facilitate a more sophisticated analysis. A tagset usually adheres to a particular descriptive or theoretical stance of language. Tagsets are often based around grammatical (part-of-speech) categories or semantic categories.

tag stripping Tags provide additional levels of information within a **corpus**, although they can make the corpus difficult for humans to read (and can also sometimes interfere with lexical analysis). As Leech (1997: 6) notes, one aspect of good practice for corpus **annotation** is that it should be possible and easy to dispense with the annotations, reverting back to the untagged corpus. Some corpus analysis software, for example **WordSmith**, allow the user to specify which tags they would like to ignore, a default case being anything that occurs within **Standard Generalised Markup Language** (SGML) bracketing <...>. See Greenbaum (1996) for a description of tag-stripping facilities with the **Corpus of English** (ICE) corpus.

tag transition probabilities The probability of some particular **part-of-speech tag** being followed by another specified tag in running text is a 'transition probability'. These are usually determined by statistical analysis of tagged **corpora**. For instance, if there are 50,000 tokens tagged NN1 in a **corpus**, and 30,000 of them are followed by tokens tagged VVZ, then the tag transition probability for NN1→VVZ is 60 per cent. In many probabilistic **taggers,** a **hidden Markov model** is used to combine tag transition probabilities to work out the likelihood of each of the potential tags for a given token being the correct tag. The process whereby tag transition probabilities are calculated for use in a tagger is called 'training' the tagger. (See also **bigram and trigram.**)

template tagger A piece of software that automatically patches (that is, corrects) **tagging** errors in a **corpus.** A template tagger was used in the final stages of tagging the **British National Corpus (BNC),** using a set of sophisticated rules in part derived by semi-automatic procedures from a sample set of texts which had previously been manually disambiguated.

term bank A special type of computer **lexicon,** containing a list of words that are technical terms in some particular field or domain. Term banks are often created from **corpora** by means of automated **terminology extraction.** Many term banks are bilingual or multilingual, making them of particular use in translation (including **machine translation),** because a word used as a technical term will often have a different translation to the same word used in normal non-technical language. An example of a multilingual term bank available on the Web is Eurodicautom (see http://europa.eu.int/eurodicautom/Controller).

terminology extraction Terminology extraction, also sometimes called 'terminology acquisition', is a type of **information extraction.** Terminology extraction software is designed to identify and create a list of words in a text or **corpus** that are likely to be technical terms, in order to create a **term bank.**

text archive see **archive**

text capture The process of gathering the texts that will comprise a **corpus**, text capture is one of a number of stages in corpus **compilation**. Text capture can involve the **scanning** or **keyboarding** of written texts, as well as **proof reading** to ensure that errors are removed. Spoken recordings need to be transcribed using an **annotation** scheme to represent particular features of conversation: speaker identification, prosody, fillers, overlap etc. Text capture should also involve the systematic backing up of data.

Text Encoding Initiative (TEI) Launched in 1987, the TEI is an international and interdisciplinary standard for representing texts electronically. It is hosted by the Universities of Oxford, Bergen and Virginia and Brown University and is sponsored by a number of bodies including the **Association for Computers and the Humanities (ACH)**, the **Association for Computational Linguistics (ACL)** and the **Association for Literary and Linguistic Computing (ALLC)**. Its guidelines for text **encoding** can be applied to any text, regardless of language, date of production or **genre**. It uses a large **tagset** that is based on both **Standard Generalised Markup Language (SGML)** and **Extensible Markup Language (XML)**. It provides an environment for creating customised **document type definitions (DTDs)**. Projects that use TEI tagging include the **British National Corpus (BNC)**, the Wittgenstein Archive, the Women Writers' Project and Perseus. See Sperberg-McQueen and Burnard (2002).

Text Segmentation for Speech (TESS) Project The project aimed to develop predictive theories about English intonation in order to make automated text-to-speech systems sound more natural. It explored **grammatical, prosodic** and **lexical** aspects of spoken English using the **London–Lund Corpus**. See Svartvik (1990a).

Text Segmentation for Speech (TESS) tagger A probabilistic **tagger** developed at Lund University that was designed to facilitate the syntactic analysis of spoken texts on the **Text Segmentation for Speech (TESS) Project**. It had an error rate of between 3 to 6 per cent, using 200 tags. See Svartvik (1990b).

text type see **genre**

Thai English Learner Corpus (TELC) A **learner corpus** consisting of over a million words of essays and exam papers produced by native speakers of Thai learning English.

Thesaurus Linguae Graecae (TLG) An on-line **archive** of texts written in ancient, classical and medieval Greek. The term also refers to the research centre that constructs and maintains the TLG. The archive contains more than 90 million words, representing nearly all the surviving literature in Greek prior to AD 1453. See http://www.tlg.uci.edu.

thinning A method of reducing the amount of information in a **concordance** so that it can be more easily analysed. For example, the word *basic* occurs 10,988 times in the **British National Corpus (BNC)**, so it would take an extremely long time to examine each instance of *basic* in the context in which it occurs. The concordance can be thinned to a more manageable level by programming the **concordancer** to present the user with, say, 100 random concordance lines.

TIGER Corpus A large German **treebank,** consisting of around 700,000 words of newspaper text. It is **annotated** for part-of-speech as a part of its **parsing markup**. It is available on the Web at http://www.ims. uni-stuttgart.de/projekte/TIGER/TIGERCorpus/.

TIMIT Acoustic–Phonetic Continuous Speech Corpus A **spoken corpus** consisting of recordings and transcriptions of ten specially-designed sentences being read by several hundred speakers.

TIPSTER Corpus A large collection of American English texts constructed for use in **information retrieval** and **information extraction.** It consists of approximately 500 million words of text from newspapers and government documents. Its **markup** is based on the **Corpus Encoding Standard (CES).**

TOEFL 2000 Spoken and Written Academic Language Corpus (T2K-SWAL) A corpus of English from academic contexts, developed at Northern Arizona University. It is around 2.8 million words in size and is notable for containing spoken academic language, for example transcribed speech from the classroom, as well as academic writing such as textbooks.

token A single linguistic unit, most often a word, although depending on the **encoding** system being used, a single word can be split into more than one token, for example *he's* (*he* + *'s*). (See also **tokenisation, type, type/token ratio.**)

tokenisation The automatic process of converting all of a text into separate **token**s, for example, by splitting conjoined words like *he's*, separating punctuation (such as commas and full stops) from words and removing capitalisation. Tokenisation is usually the first stage in **lemmatisation** or **part-of-speech tagging**.

tool A term given to any piece of software that can automatically manipulate electronic (usually textual) data. Some tools can be used in the **compilation** of **corpora**, for example, by collecting files from the internet. Other tools are used to **encode corpus** data, such as **part-of-speech taggers**, while other tools carry out analysis on the data, generating **frequency** information, **concordances**, **keywords**, **collocations** or carrying out statistical tests.

Tools for Syntactic Corpus Analysis (TOSCA) Corpus The TOSCA Corpus contains 1.5 million words of English, stored in the **Nijmegen Linguistic Database** (see Oostdijk 1991).

training corpus A collection of text (often a smaller, representative sample taken from a larger **corpus**) that has been **annotated** and can be used to 'train' an automatic **tagger** or **parser** to apply that same **annotation** to other texts. The tagger is then tested by using it to tag a blank version of (part of) the training corpus, which is then analysed for errors. This provides feedback that is used to refine and improve the accuracy of the tagger.

TRAINS Dialogue Corpus A **spoken corpus** created in the early 1990s from recordings of dialogues produced by pairs of participants in problem-solving interactions. The texts are available at http://www.cs.rochester.edu/research/cisd/resources/trains.html.

treebank A **corpus** that has been grammatically **annotated**

in order to identify and label different constituent structures or phrases. Because of the system of labelling (Figure 3 shows a visual representation), such structures are sometimes referred to as 'trees'.

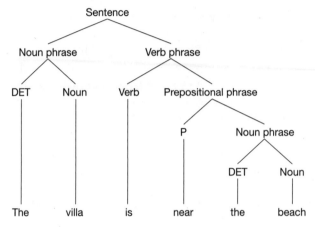

Fig. 3. Visual representation of a treebank:
DET = Determiner, P = Preposition

TreeTagger A **part-of-speech tagger** developed at the University of Stuttgart. While it is based on **probabilistic disambiguation,** unlike most probabilistic taggers it does not use a **hidden Markov model.** Instead, the likeliest tag is selected using a 'decision tree'. The TreeTagger is language-independent and has been trained to tag a number of different languages, including German, English, French and Spanish. It also provides **lemmatisation** in its output. See http://www.ims.uni-stuttgart.de/ projekte/corplex/TreeTagger/DecisionTreeTagger.html.

Trésor de la Langue Française Informatisé (TLFi) A **database** consisting of 170 million words of written French from the seventeenth century to the present, from about

2,600 texts. Genres include novels, verse, journalism, essays, correspondence and treatises. Standard scholarly editions were used to convert the text into machine-readable form.

trigram see **bigram and trigram**

Trigrams'n'Tags (TnT) A **part-of-speech tagger** created by Thosten Brants at the Universität des Saarlandes, Germany. It is a **language independent tagger** and can be used with any **tagset**. It is optimised for speed and for training on a large variety of **corpora**.

type While the number of **token**s in a **corpus** refers to the total number of words, the number of types refers to the total number of *unique* words. For example, the word *ship* may occur 177 times in a corpus, but it only counts as one type of word. Types are used in calculating the **type/token ratio** (a measure of lexical repetition) of a text or corpus.

type/token ratio The number of **types** (unique words) in a text, divided by the number of **tokens** (total number of words) and expressed as a percentage. A high type/token ratio suggests that a text is lexically diverse, whereas a low type/token ratio suggests that there is a lot of repetition of lexical items in a file.

The type/token ratio tends to use all of the words in a text, unlike measures of **lexical density** which can remove the **function words**. However, the larger the **corpus** or file is, the lower the type/token ratio will be, due to the repetitive nature of function words. One solution is therefore to calculate a **standardised type/token ratio**.

| U |

UCREL Semantic Analysis System (USAS) A **semantic tagger**, that is to say a software system for undertaking the automatic semantic analysis of text. The semantic **tagset** used by USAS was originally loosely based on Tom McArthur's *Longman Lexicon of Contemporary English* (McArthur, 1981). It has a multi-tier structure with twenty-one major discourse fields, subdivided, and with the possibility of further fine-grained subdivision in certain cases. For example, the code T3 refers to 'Time: Old, new and young; age', so the word *kids* is assigned T3- placing it at one end of a linear scale, whereas a word like *pensioner* would receive T3+. In addition, when words can fit into more than one semantic category, they may receive more than one semantic tag, shown by a forward slash sign. So *kids* is tagged as T3-/S2mf which also places it in the category of 'People'. See the **University Centre for Computer Corpus Research on Language (UCREL)**.

Unicode Unicode is a large **character set** covering most of the world's writing systems, offering a way of standardising the hundreds of different **encoding** systems for rendering electronic text in different languages, which were often conflicting. Older character sets such as the **American Standard Code for Information Exchange (ASCII)** used 8-bit encoding (meaning that they can only represent 256 characters) so no single system was adequate for all the letters, punctuation and other symbols in common use. Therefore, character sets based around different languages would be incompatible with one another – a character rendered as ă in one character set could appear as something completely different in another, and mixing writing systems in a single character set would be impossible. Unicode, on the other hand, uses a 16-bit or 32-bit encoding system, allowing for thousands of unique characters. Many modern **corpora** are encoded in Unicode (for instance the **Enabling Minority Language Engineering (EMILLE) Corpus** and the **Lancaster Corpus of Mandarin Chinese (LCMC)**).

Universidad Autónoma de Madrid (UAM) Spanish Treebank A **parsed corpus** (or **treebank**) of 1,500 sentences in Spanish. (See also http://www.lllf.uam.es/~sandoval/UAMTreebank.html.)

University Centre for Computer Corpus Research on Language (UCREL) A research centre at Lancaster University that focuses on corpus building and exploitation of Modern English, Early Modern English, modern foreign languages, minority, endangered and ancient languages. UCREL holds a conference every two years and has been involved in the creation and **annotation** of corpora such as the **British National Corpus (BNC)**, the **Enabling Minority Language Engineering Corpus (EMILLE)** and the **Lancaster Corpus of Mandarin Chinese (LCMC)**. UCREL also developed the **CLAWS part-of-speech tagger**, the **UCREL semantic analysis system (USAS)** and the **Automatic Content Analysis of Spoken Discourse (ACASD) word sense tagging system.**

UNIX A computer operating system. Many **corpus** analysis **tools** have been designed to run on mainframe computers in a Unix environment, which users might access via a network. This is because, until the mid to late 1980s, the large **size** of many **corpora** meant that a very fast, powerful computer was required to process them in a reasonable length of time. However, as desktop computers become more powerful, tools designed to run on common PC operating systems such as Windows or Linux are capable of processing larger and larger corpora with ease.

unrestricted text In **computational linguistics**, a common goal is to develop methods and **tools** that will work on unrestricted text, that is, any text at all in a given language. Many **part-of-speech taggers**, for instance, can process unrestricted text (albeit with some errors). If the text to be analysed is restricted – that is, drawn from a defined type of text whose language does not vary a great deal, for example computer manuals or recipe books – it is often easier to develop tools, but the tools are obviously of much wider use if they can handle un-restricted text.

upward collocation A form of **collocation** outlined by Sinclair (1991: 115–19) whereby the focus is upon *grammatical* patterns surrounding a particular lexical item. Upward collocation occurs when one collocate occurs more frequently in a **corpus** or text than its collocational pair. Upward collocates tend to be **function words** rather than **content words**. For example, upward collocates of the word *bachelor* (which occurs 1,135 times in the **British National Corpus (BNC)**) are *who* (200,991 occurrences in the BNC), *a* (21,69,250), *his* (409,826) and *into* (157,875). (See also **colligation, downward collocation**.)

V

validity A variable or measure is valid if its values are close to the true values of the thing that the variable or measure represents. Validity is therefore an important aspect of **corpus design,** related to the concept of **representativeness.**

Varbrul programs The name given to a group of analysis **tools** including *GoldVarb* and *Varbrul for MS-DOS.* These programs are used to conduct a type of statistical analysis called a 'variable rule analysis or multivariate analysis' on **corpus** data or other large quantity of language **data.** This analysis tries to identify whether different linguistic variables in the data are related to one another, that is if changes in one variable coincide with or correspond to changes in another variable.

variation Many studies using **corpora** have focused on variation by comparing two or more dialects, channels, **genres,** languages or varieties of language in order to uncover the main differences and similarities between them (see also **multi-dimensional analysis** (Biber 1988, 1989)). Other studies of note include Altenberg's (1994) comparison of spoken and written English, Leech and Fallon's (1992) study of British and American English, Rissanen's (1992) diachronic comparison of the **Helsinki Corpus** texts and Gillard and Gadsby's (1998) comparison of learner English and native speaker English.

Viterbi algorithm A technique for **probabilistic disambiguation** using a **hidden Markov model.** One problem with using a Markov model for **part-of-speech tagging** is that it can need a lot of computer power. For example, if we have a sequence of five tokens, each with five potential tags, then the number of possible sequences is $5 \times 5 \times 5 \times 5 \times 5 = 3,125$. Calculating the probability of each of these sequences requires lots of memory and computing. If the Viterbi algorithm is used to process the Markov model, however, unlikely sequences are dropped from consideration as the program goes along, and the computer only has to take a small number of good possibilities into account at any one time. The **VOLSUNGA** tagger is based on this type of Markov model system.

VocabProfile An MS-DOS-based **tool** which compares vocabulary overlap between different texts. It also compares texts to a pre-specified **frequency** list and calculates the proportion of the text that is made from the words in the list. It can be useful in determining whether a text contains language that is representative of a particular **genre**. See Laufer and Nation (1995).

VOLSUNGA A probabilistic **tagger** created by De Rose (1988). It has ninety-seven tags and achieved 96 per cent accuracy when tagging the **Brown Corpus**. Its method of tagging involves using dynamic programming (Dano 1975) to choose an optimal path – one whose component **collocations** multiplied out to the highest probability. (See also **Viterbi algorithm**.)

W

Web as corpus see **World Wide Web**

Wellington Corpus of Spoken New Zealand English (WSC) A **corpus** consisting of a million words of spoken New Zealand English that was collected between 1988 and 1994 by the Victoria University of Wellington. It contains 2,000 word extracts, consisting of 75 per cent informal speech, 12 per cent formal and 12 per cent semi-formal speech) as well as monologues and dialogues. See Holmes et al. (1998).

Wellington Corpus of Written New Zealand English (WWC)

A **corpus** consisting of a million words of written New Zealand English collected from writings published in the years 1986 to 1990. Its structure mirrors the categories in the **Brown Corpus,** containing 2,000 word excerpts of a range of texts. See Bauer (1993).

wild card A character that can stand for any other character in a **regular expression**. Wild cards allow more sophisticated searches in **corpora** to be carried out. For example, a **concordance** program could specify that the * character acted as a wild card, standing in for a string of any characters of any length. It would be possible to search for any word that begins with the word *look* (for example *looked, looking, looker*) by carrying out a search on the string *look**. Other types of wild cards can represent any single character – the full stop character can often function this way in search syntax, for example h.t will find *hat, hit, hot* and *hut.* Different concordance **tools** may use different (or no) wildcards in their search facilities.

Wmatrix An analysis system for English texts and **corpora** developed by Paul Rayson at Lancaster University. It is accessed using a web-based interface. As well as tagging text using the **CLAWS part-of-speech** tagger and the **UCREL Semantic Analysis System (USAS)** semantic tagger, Wmatrix functions as a **concordancer**. It can also calculate **keywords**, key part of speech tags, and key semantic categories in a text.

Wolverhampton Business English Corpus (WBE) A **corpus** of 10 million words of English texts drawn from the World Wide Web, and consisting entirely of documents from the domain of business.

word list A list of all of the words that appear in a text or **corpus,** often useful for dictionary creation. Word lists often give the frequencies of each word (or **token**) in the corpus. Words are most usually ordered alphabetically, or in terms of **frequency,** either with a raw frequency count and/or the percentage that the word contributes towards the whole text. Additionally, word lists can be **lemmatised** or **annotated** with part-of-speech or semantic information (including probabilities – for example, the word *house* occurs as a noun about 99 per cent of the time and as a verb 1 per cent of the time). Word lists are needed when calculating **key words** and **key key words.** (See also **lexicon.**)

WordCruncher A **corpus tool** that provides text indexing and retrieval software for text analysis created by Brigham Young University. It includes two separate and distinct programs, WCView and WCIndex. WCIndex indexes texts to be studied with WCView; WCView analyses and retrieves texts prepared with WCIndex. Users may catalogue and alphabetically sort each word in a text, written in English or other languages, into a WordCruncher Index. They can also analyse and manipulate **data** from a textbase in any number of ways, carrying out searches on words, phrases, **regular expressions** etc. WordCruncher also allows analysis of **frequency distributions** and can create **word lists, collocations** and **concordances.** It is available from Johnston and Company, Electronic Publishers, Indiana.

WordSmith Tools A software package for analysing the lexis of texts and **corpora,** developed by Mike Scott. It can be used to produce **frequency** lists, to run **concordance** searches and calculate **collocations** for particular words, and to find **keywords** in a text and examine their distribution. It can be used with both **plain text** and text with **markup** tags (for instance **Standard Generalised Markup Language**). Unlike some other analysis packages (for example **SARA, WordCruncher**) WordSmith does not require the **corpus** to be **indexed** in advance. (See also www.lexically.net/wordsmith.)

World Wide Web More commonly WWW or simply 'the Web', this is a global network of interlinked hypertext documents that can be read using a browser program and an Internet connection. At the beginning of the twenty-first century it has become the main way of accessing resources on the Internet. The explosive growth of the Web in the last years of the twentieth century means that it is now an immense mass of text, numbering in the billions of documents, and greater in size than even the largest **corpus** by a factor of thousands. This being the case, researchers such as Kilgarriff and Grefenstette (2003) have investigated the possibility of using the web as a corpus. This is particularly useful for **lexicography**, since most words occur only rarely (see **Zipf's Law**); a huge dataset is needed to get a reasonable set of examples of such words.

At a basic level, **frequency** counts for words on the Web can be obtained using a commercial search engine such as Google (www.google.com). At a more sophisticated level, software has been developed to make using the Web as a corpus more like using a 'normal' corpus: for example, the WebCorp **concordancer** (http://www.webcorp.org.uk), WebCONC (http://www.niederlandistik.fu-berlin.de/cgi-bin/web-conc.cgi), or WebKWiC (http://miniappolis.com/WebKWiC/WebKWiCHome.html). Quite apart from using the whole Web as a corpus, the Web has frequently been employed as an inexpensive and convenient method to gather documents for inclusion in a corpus. Some **corpora** can also be obtained and/or analysed via a Web interface; see **BNCweb, on-line corpora**.

While the Web's **size** is its great strength as a corpus, its great drawback is the low level of control that researchers have over its contents. So, if **representativeness** or a careful corpus **design** are important for a particular **corpus-based** study, the Web would not be the best corpus to use.

written corpus A **corpus** that only contains texts that have been produced or published in written format. This could include traditional books, novels, textbooks, newspapers, magazines or unpublished letters and diaries. It could also include written texts that were produced electronically; for example, emails, bulletin board contributions and websites. The criteria for what exactly constitutes a written text can have grey areas – for example, prepared speeches or television/film/radio scripts are probably better considered as written-to-be-spoken texts. In the absence of a pre-existing electronic version, written texts need to be **scanned** or **keyboarded**. Because written texts tend to be grammatically predictable, many **taggers** usually perform with a higher accuracy on written texts than spoken texts (particularly spontaneous conversations). Written **corpora** generally tend to contain a higher number of conjunctions and prepositions than spoken data, suggesting longer, more complex sentences.

X

Xerox tagger A probabilistic **part-of-speech tagger** based on a **hidden Markov model**. It can be trained on untagged **data** using the **Baum–Welch algorithm**. It was originally trained to tag English, but as it is **language-independent,** it has also been retrained for other languages, for instance Spanish. See Cutting et al. (1992).

XHTML A form of **HTML** which complies with the rules of **XML**, rather than the rules of **SGML**, the basis for HTML. XHTML was designed in the early years of the twenty-first century as a successor to HTML.

Xkwic A search and retrieval **tool**, also called CQp, that was developed at the University of Stuttgart. It is capable of rapid, complex searches on very large **corpora** and can also carry out **frequency** distributions and calculate **collocates** based on **part-of-speech tagged** corpora. It is free and runs on **Unix**, Linux and **Java** platforms. See Christ et al. (1999).

XML Aware Indexing and Retrieval Architecture (Xaira) A software package descended from **SARA**, and with many of the same capabilities, for example running queries for words, **markup,** or word tags to produce **concordances.** But while SARA was designed specifically for use with the **British National Corpus (BNC)**, Xaira can be used with any text or **corpus** that is **encoded** in **XML**. Xaira has full **Unicode** support, allowing it to be used with **corpora** in any language and any writing system. Like SARA, Xaira searches large corpora quickly by looking through an **index**, which must be set up in advance for each corpus. See http://www.xaira.org.

Y

York–Toronto–Helsinki Corpus of Old English Prose (YCOE) This **historical corpus** contains 1.5 million words of text from the Anglo-Saxon period. It has been syntactically **annotated** (see **parsing**), with an annotation scheme which is the same as that of the **Penn–Helsinki Parsed Corpus of Middle English**. It was developed alongside a corpus of poetry from the same period, the *York–Helsinki Parsed Corpus of Old English Poetry*. Together with the Penn–Helsinki **corpora**, these form a family of parsed historical corpora.

Z

Zipf's law The mathematical formula that describes the **frequency** patterns found for words in **corpora**. In any **corpus** (and in language as a whole), there are a small number of words that occur very frequently: for instance, *of*, *the*, or *it*. But there are many, many words that occur very infrequently: for example *destructiveness*, *elephantine*, *pseudonymous*. If word **frequency** is plotted on a graph against the number of words in the corpus that occur with that frequency, the points form a characteristic curve whose shape is described by Zipf's law. This is an interesting finding, because Zipf's law also describes the distribution of many things other than words. For example, it has been found that the popularity of websites follows the same pattern (a very few are very popular, and an immensely greater number are viewed by hardly anyone at all). (See also **hapax legomena**.)

Zürich English Newspaper Corpus (ZEN) This **historical corpus** consists of early English newspapers from the period 1671 to 1791, and contains more than 1 million words of text in **Standard Generalised Markup Language (SGML)** format.

Z-score A statistical measure of the degree of relatedness of two elements: it expresses how unlikely it is that the two words are unrelated. In **corpus linguistics,** it is often used as a measure of the strength of a **collocation** between two words.

References

Aijmer, K. (2002) *English discourse particles: Evidence from a corpus*, Amsterdam: Benjamins.

Altenberg (1994) 'On the functions of such in spoken and written English', in N. Oostdijk and P. de Haan (eds), *Corpus-based research into language: In honour of Jan Aarts*, Amersterdam: Rodopi, pp. 223–40.

Anderson, A. H., Bader, M., Bard, E., Boyle, E., Doherty, G. M., Garrod, S., Isard, S., Kowtko, J., McAllister, J., Miller, J., Sotillo, C., Thompson, H. S. and Weinert, R. (1991) 'The HCRC map task corpus', *Language and speech* 34: 4, 351–66.

Aston, G. and Burnard, L. (1998) *The BNC handbook: Exploring the British national corpus with SARA*, Edinburgh: Edinburgh University Press.

Atkins, B. T. S., Clear, J. and Ostler, N. (1992) 'Corpus design criteria', *Literary and linguistic computing* 7: 1, 1–16.

Atwell, E., Howarth, P. and Souter, C. (2003) 'The ISLE corpus: Italian and German spoken learner's English', *ICAME journal* 27: 5–18.

Baker, M. (1993) 'Corpus linguistics and translation studies: implications and applications', in M. Baker, G. Francis and E. Tognini-Bonelli (eds), *Text and technology: In honour of John Sinclair*, Amsterdam: Benjamins, pp. 233–52.

Baker, P. (1997) 'Consistency and accuracy in correcting automatically tagged data', in R. Garside, G. Leech and A. McEnery (eds), *Corpus annotation: Linguistic information from computer text corpora*, London: Longman, pp. 243–50.

Baker, P., Hardie, A., McEnery, A., Xiao, R., Bontcheva, K., Cunningham, H., Gaizauskas, R., Hamza, O., Maynard, D., Tablan, V., Ursu, C., Jayaram, B. D. and Leisher, M. (2004) 'Corpus linguistics and South Asian languages: corpus creation and tool development', in *Literary and linguistic computing* 19: 4, 509–24.

Banerjee, S. and Pedersen, T. (2003) 'The design, implementation, and use of the Ngram statistics package', in *Proceedings of the fourth international conference on intelligent text processing and computational linguistics*, 17–21 February 2003, Mexico City, pp. 370–81.

Barlow, M. (1998) *A corpus of spoken professional American English*. Houston, TX: Athelstan.

Bauer, L. (1993) *Manual of information to accompany the Wellington corpus of written New Zealand English*, Wellington: Department of Linguistics, Victoria University of Wellington.

Beal, J. C. and Corrigan, K. O. (2000) 'A "time-capsule" for future generations: the *Newcastle–Poitiers corpus of Tyneside English*', Paper presented at *Sociolinguistics symposium*, University of the West of England, Bristol, April 2000 (n.p.).

Beale, A. (1987) 'Towards a distributional lexicon', in R. Garside, G. Leech and G. Sampson (eds), *The computational analysis of English: A corpus based approach*, London: Longman.

Bernadini, S. (2000) *Competence, capacity, corpora*, Bologna: CLUEB.

Berry-Rogghe, G. L. E. (1973) 'The computation of collocations and their relevance in lexical studies', in A. J. Aitken, R. Bailey and N. Hamilton-Smith (eds), *The computer and literary studies*, Edinburgh: Edinburgh University Press.

Biber, D. (1988) *Variation across speech and writing*, Cambridge: Cambridge University Press.

Biber, D. (1989) 'A typology of English texts', *Linguistics* 27: 3–43.

Biber, D. (1990) 'Methodological issues regarding corpus-based analyses of linguistic variation', *Literary and linguistic computing* 5: 257–69.

Biber, D. (1993) 'Representativeness in corpus design', *Literary and linguistic computing* 8: 4, 243–57.

Biber, D. (1998) *Corpus linguistics: Investigating language structure and use*, Cambridge: Cambridge University Press.

Biber, D., Conrad, S. and Reppen, R. (1994a) 'Corpus-based approaches to issues in applied linguistics', *Applied linguistics* 15:2, 169–89.

Biber, D., Finegan. E. and Atkinson, D. (1994b) 'ARCHER and its challenges: Compiling and exploring a representative corpus of historical English registers', in U. Fries, G. Tottie and P. Schneider (eds), *Creating and using English language corpora. Papers from the fourteenth international conference on English language research on computerized corpora, Zürich 1993*. Amsterdam and Atlanta, GA: Rodopi, pp. 1–3.

Biber, D., Johansson, S., Leech, G., Conrad, S., and Finnegan, E. (1999) *Longman grammar of spoken and written English*, London: Longman.

Bick, E. (2000) *The parsing system 'Palvaras' – Automatic grammatical analysis of Portuguese in a constraint grammar framework*, Århus: Århus University Press.

Bongers, H. (1947) *The history and principles of vocabulary control*, Worden: Wocopi.

Brill, E. (1992) 'A simple rule-based part-of-speech tagger', in *Proceedings of ANLP*, Trento/Italy: ACL, pp. 152–5.

Bryan, M. T. (1988) *SGML – An author's guide to the standard generalised markup language*, Wokingham: Addison-Wesley.

Boualem, A-M., Harié, S. and Véronis, J. (1996) 'MtScript: un éditeur de textes multilingues', *3ème colloque Africain sur la recherche en informatique* (CARI'96), Libreville, Gabon, pp. 262–71.

Butler, C. S. (1985) *Computers in linguistics*, Oxford: Blackwell.

Burnard, L. (1995) *Users reference guide for the British national corpus*, Oxford: Oxford University Computing Services.

Carletta, J. and Isard, A. (1999) 'The MATE annotation workbench: user requirements', in *Proceedings of the ACL workshop: towards standards and tools for discourse tagging*, University of Maryland, June 1999, pp. 11–17.

Chafe, W., DuBois, J. and Thompson, S. (1991) 'Towards a new corpus of spoken American English', in K. Aijmer and B. Altenberg (eds), *English Corpus Linguistics*, London: Longman.

Chomsky, N. (1957) *Syntactic structures*, The Hague: Mouton.

Chomsky, N. (1965) *Aspects of the theory of syntax*, Cambridge, MA: MIT Press.

Chomsky, N. (1968) *Language and mind*. New York: Harcourt Brace.

Christ, O. (1994) 'A modular and flexible architecture for an integrated corpus query system', *Proceedings of COMPLEX'94: 3rd conference on computational lexicography and text research* (7–10 July 1994), Budapest, Hungary, pp. 23–32.

Christ, O., Schulze, B., Hofmann, A. and König, E. (1999) *The IMS corpus workbench: Corpus query processor (CQP) user's manual*, Stuttgart: Institute for Natural Language Processing, University of Stuttgart.

Church, K. W. and Liberman, M. (1991) 'A status report on the ACL/DCI', in *Using corpora*, Proceedings from the new OED conference. Waterloo, Ontario: University of Waterloo Centre for the New OED and Text Research, pp. 84–91.

Claridge, C. (1997) 'A century in the life of multi-word verbs', in M. Ljung (ed.), *Corpus-based studies in English. Papers from the 17th international conference on English language research on computerized corpora*, Amsterdam and Atlanta: Rodopi, pp. 69–85.

Clarkson, P. R. and Rosenfeld, R. (1997) 'Statistical language modeling using the CMU–Cambridge Toolkit', from *Proceedings ESCA Eurospeech 1997*, pp. 2707–10.

Clear, J., Fox, G., Francis, G., Krishnamurthy, R. and Moon, R. (1996) 'Cobuild: the state of the art', *International journal of corpus linguistics* 1: 303–14.

Collins, P. and Peters, P. (1988) 'The Australian corpus project', in M. Kyto, O. Ihalainen and M. Risanen (eds), *Corpus linguistics, hard and soft*, Amsterdam: Rodopi, pp. 103–20.

Connolly, D. (1995) *Character set considered harmful*. Internet-draft [draft-ietf-html-charset-harmful-00.txt], Internet Engineering Task Force (IETF), HTML working group (HTML-WG).

Coulthard, M. (1993) 'On beginning the study of forensic texts: corpus concordance collocation', in M. Hoey (ed.), *Data, description, discourse*, London: HarperCollins.

Cunningham, H. (2002) 'GATE, a general architecture for text engineering', *Computers and the humanities* 36: 223–54.

Cutting, D., Kupiec, J., Pedersen, J. and Sibun, P. (1992) 'A practical part-of-speech tagger', in *Proceedings of ANLP-92*, Trento, Italy.

Daelmans, W. (1995) 'Memory-based lexical acquisition and process-ing', in P. Steffens (ed.), *Machine translation and the lexicon, lecture notes in artificial intelligence*, Springer-Verlag, Berlin, pp. 85–98.

Daelmans, W., Zavrel, J., Berck, P. and Gillis, S. (1996) 'MBT: a memory-based part of speech tagger-generator', in E. Ejerhed and I. Dagan (eds), *Proceedings of the fourth workshop on very large corpora*, University of Copenhagen, Denmark, pp. 14–27.

Dano, S. (1975) *Nonlinear and dynamic programming*, New York: Springer-Verlag.

Davidson, L. (1992) 'Using large text data-banks on computers', in P. Roach (ed.), *Computing in linguistics and phonetics: Introductory readings*, London: Academic Press, pp. 5–34.

Davies, M. (2000) 'Using multi-million word corpora of historical and dialectal Spanish texts to teach advanced courses in Spanish linguis-tics', in L. Burnard, T. McEnery and P. Lang (eds), *Rethinking language pedagogy from a corpus perspective*, Frankfurt: Peter Lang, pp. 173–85.

de Haan, P. (1984) 'Problem-oriented tagging of English corpus data', in J. Aarts and W. Meijs (eds), *Corpus linguistics*, Amsterdam: Rodopi, pp. 123–39.

de Haan, P. (1989) *Postmodifying clauses in the English noun phrase. A corpus-based study*, Amsterdam: Rodopi.

Denison, David (1984) 'A corpus of late modern English prose', in M. Kytö, M. Rissanen and S. Wright (eds), *Corpora across the centuries. Proceedings of the first international colloquium on*

English diachronic corpora, St Catharine's College Cambridge, 25–27 March 1993, Amsterdam and Atlanta, GA: Rodopi, pp. 7–16.

de Rose, S. J. (1988) 'Grammatical category disambiguation by statistical optimization', *Computational linguistics* 14: 1, 31–9.

Di Eugenio, Jordan, P. W. and Pylkkanen, L. (1998) *The COCONUT project: dialogue annotation manual*. ISP Technical Report 98–1, University of Pittsburgh.

Dunning, T. (1993) 'Accurate methods for the statistics of surprise and coincidence', *Computational linguistics* 19: 1, 61–74.

Eaton, H. (1940) *Semantic frequency list for English, French, German and Spanish*, Chicago: Chicago University Press.

Edwards, J. A. (1993) 'Survey of electronic corpora and related resources for language researchers', in J. A. Edwards and M. D. Lampert (eds), *Talking data: Transcription and coding in discourse research*, Hillsdale: Lawrence Erlbaum, pp. 263–310.

Eyes, E. and Leech, G. (1993) 'Syntactic annotation: Linguistic aspects of grammatical tagging and skeleton parsing', in E. Black, R. Garside and G. Leech (eds), *Statistically-driven computer grammars of English: The IBM/Lancaster Approach*, Amsterdam: Rodopi, pp. 36–61.

Fang, A. C. (1996) 'AUTASYS: Grammatical tagging and cross-tagset mapping', in *Comparing English worldwide: The international corpus of English*, S. Greenbaum (ed.), Oxford: Oxford University Press, pp. 110–24.

Fillmore, C. J. (1985) 'Frames and the semantics of understanding', *Quaderni di Semantica*, 6: 2, 222–54.

Firth, J. (1957) *Papers in linguistics 1934–1951*, London: Oxford University Press.

Fligelstone, S. (1992) 'Developing a scheme for annotating text to show anaphoric relations', in G. Leitner (ed.), *New directions in English language corpora. Methology, results, software developments*, Berlin: Mouton de Gruyter, 153–70.

Francis, W. N. and Kučera, H. (1964) *Manual of information to accompany 'A standard sample of present-day edited American English, for use with digital computers'* (revised 1979). Providence, RI: Department of Linguistics, Brown University.

Francis, W. N. and Kučera, H. (1982) *Frequency analysis of English usage: Lexicon and grammar*, Boston: Houghton Mifflin.

Fries, C. (1940) *American English grammar*, Monograph 10, New York: National Council of Teachers of English.

Fries, C. (1952) *The structure of English*, London: Longman.

Fries, C. and Traver, A. (1940) *English word lists. A study of their adaptability and instruction*, Washington, DC: American Council of

Education.

Gaizauskas, R., Foster, J., Wilks, Y., Arundel, J., Clough, P. and Piao, S. (2001) 'The METER corpus: a corpus for analysing journalistic text reuse', in *Proceedings of the corpus linguistics 2001 conference*, Lancaster, UK, pp. 214–23.

Garnham, A., Shillock, R., Brown, G., Mill, A. and Cutler, A. (1981) 'Slips of the tongue in the London–Lund corpus of spontaneous conversation', *Linguistics* 19: 805–17.

Garside, R. (1987) 'The CLAWS Word-tagging System', in R. Garside, G. Leech and G. Sampson (eds), *The computational analysis of English: A corpus-based approach*, London: Longman.

Garside, R. (1996) 'The robust tagging of unrestricted text: The BNC experience', in J. Thomas and M. Short (eds), *Using corpora for language research: Studies in the Honour of Geoffrey Leech*, Longman, London, pp. 167–80.

Garside, R. and Smith, N. (1997) 'A hybrid grammatical tagger: CLAWS4', in R. Garside, G. Leech and A. McEnery (eds), *Corpus annotation: Linguistic information from computer text corpora*, Longman, London, pp. 102–21.

Gazdar, G., Klein, E., Pullum, G. K. and Sag, I. A. (1985) *Generalized phrase structure grammar*, Oxford: Blackwell.

George, H. V. (1963) 'A verb form frequency count', *ELT journal* 18: 1, 31–7.

Gillard, Patrick and Gadsby, Adam (1998) 'Using a learners' corpus in compiling ELT dictionaries', in S. Granger (ed.), *Learner English on computer*, London: Longman, pp. 159–71.

Goldfarb, C. (1990) *The SGML handbook*, Oxford: Clarendon Press.

Grabe, E. and Post, B. (2002) 'Intonational Variation in English', in B. Bel and I. Marlin (eds), *Proceedings of the speech prosody 2002 conference* (11–13 April 2002), Aix-en-Provence: Laboratoire Parole et Language, pp. 343–6.

Granger, S. (ed.) (1998) *Learner English on computer*, London: Longman.

Granger, S., Hung, J. and Petch-Tyson, S. (eds) (2002a) *Computer learner corpora, second language acquisition and foreign language teaching*, Amsterdam: John Benjamins.

Granger S., Dagneaux E. and Meunier F. (2002b) *The international corpus of learner English. Handbook and CD-ROM*, Louvain-la-Neuve: Presses Universitaires de Louvain.

Greenbaum, S. (1991) 'ICE: the International Corpus of English', *English today* 28: 3–7.

Greenbaum, S. (1996) *Comparing English worldwide: The international corpus of English*, Oxford: Clarendon Press.

Greene, B. B. and Rubin, G. M. (1971) *Automatic grammatical tagging of English*, Providence RI: Department of Linguistics, Brown University.

Hickey, R. (1993). 'Corpus data processing with Lexa', *ICAME journal* 17: 73–96.

Hines, P. (1995) 'The Newdigate letters', *ICAME journal* 19: 158–61.

Hoffman, S. and Lehmann, H. M. (2000) 'Collocational evidence from the British national corpus', in J. Kirk (ed.), *Corpora galore: analyses and techniques in describing English*, Amsterdam: Rodopi, pp. 17–32.

Holmes, J., Vine, B. and Johnson, G. (1998) *Guide to the Wellington corpus of spoken New Zealand English*, Victoria University of Wellington, Wellington.

Homan, R. (1991) *The ethics of social research*, London: Longman.

Hunston, S. (2002) *Corpora in applied linguistics*, Cambridge: Cambridge University Press.

Hunston, S. and Francis, G. (1999) *Pattern grammar. A corpus-driven approach to the lexical grammar of English*, Amsterdam, Philadelphia: Benjamins.

Ide, N. and Véronis, J. (1994) 'MULTEXT (multilingual tools and corpora)', *Proceedings of the 14th international conference on computational linguistics, COLING '94*, Kyoto, Japan 1994, pp. 90–6.

Ingram, D. (1989) *First language acquisition*, Cambridge University Press, Cambridge.

James, C. (1992) 'Awareness, consciousness and language contrast', in C. Mair and M. Markus (eds), *New departures in contrastive linguistics*, pp. 183–97.

Jarvinen, T. (1994) 'Annotating 200 million words: the Bank of English project', in *The 15th international conference on computational linguistics proceedings*, Kyoto, pp. 565–8.

Johansson, S. (1980) 'The LOB corpus of British English texts: presentation and comments', *ALLC journal* 1: 25–36.

Johns, T. (1997) 'Contexts: the background, development and trialling of a concordance-based CALL program', in A. Wichmann, S. Fligelstone, G. Knowles and A. McEnery (eds), *Teaching and language corpora*, London: Longman, pp. 100–15.

Käding, J. (1897) *Häufigkeitswörterbuch der deutschen Sprache*, Steglitz: privately published.

Karlsson (1994) 'Robost parsing of unconstrained text', in N. Oostdijk and P. de Haan (eds), *Corpus-based research into language: In honour of Jan Aarts*, Amsterdam: Rodopi, pp. 121–42.

Kennedy, G. (1998) *An introduction to corpus linguistics*, London:

Longman.

Kilgarriff, A. and Grefenstette, G. (2003) 'Web as corpus', *Computational linguistics* 29: 3, 1–15.

Kilgarriff, A. and Tugwell, D. (2001) 'WASP-bench: An MT lexicographers' workstation supporting state-of-the-art lexical disambiguation', Proceedings of MT Summit VII, Santiago de Compostela, pp. 187–90.

Kirk, J. M. (1992) 'The Northern Ireland transcribed corpus of speech', in G. Leitner (ed.), *New directions in English language corpora*, Berlin: Mouton de Gruyter, pp. 65–73.

Knowles, G. (1993) 'The machine-readable spoken English corpus', in J. Aarts, P. de Haan and N. Oostdijk (eds), *English language corpora: Design, analysis and exploitation*, Amsterdam: Rodopi, pp. 107–22.

Kobayasi, Y., Tokunaga, T. and Tanaka, H. (1994) 'Analysis of Japanese compound nouns using collocational information', in *Proceedings of COLING-94*, Kyoto, Japan, pp. 865–9.

Kovarik, J. (2000) 'How should a large corpus be built? – A comparative study of closure in annotated newspaper corpora from two Chinese sources, towards building a larger representative corpus merged from representative sublanguage collections', Paper presented at *NAACL–ANLP 2000 workshop: Syntactic and Semantic Complexity in Natural Language Processing Systems* (n.p.).

Kurohashi, S., and Nagao, M. (1998) 'Building a Japanese parsed corpus while improving the parsing system', *Proceedings of the first international conference on language resources and evaluation, Granada, Spain*, pp. 719–24.

Kytö, M. (1991) *Manual to the diachronic part of the Helsinki corpus of English texts*, Helsinki: Department of English: University of Helsinki.

Kytö, M. (1992) 'A supplement to the Helsinki corpus of English texts: The corpus of early American English', in J. Aarts, P. Haan and N. Oostdijk (eds), *English Language corpora: Design, analysis and exploitation*, Amsterdam: Rodopi.

Kytö, M. and Rissanen, M. (1992) 'A language in transition: The Helsinki corpus of English texts', *ICAME journal* 16: 7–27.

Labov, V. (1969) 'The logic of non-standard English', *Georgetown monographs on language and linguistics* 22: 1–31.

Lancashire, I. (1991) *The humanities computing yearbook 1989/1990: A comprehensive guide to software and other resources*, Oxford: Clarendon Press.

Laufer, B. and Nation, I. S. P. (1995) 'Vocabulary size and use: Lexical richness in L2 written production', *Applied linguistics* 16: 3, 307–22.

Leech, G. (1991) 'The state of the art in corpus linguistics', in K. Aijmer and B. Altenberg (eds), *English corpus linguistics: Studies in honour of Jan Svartvik*, London: Longman, pp. 105–22.

Leech, G. (1997) 'Introducing corpus annotation', in R. Garside, G. Leech and A. McEnery (eds), *Corpus annotation: Linguistic information from computer text corpora*, London: Longman, pp. 1–18.

Leech, G. (2002) 'Recent grammatical change in English: data, description, theory', in K. Aijmer and B. Altenberg (eds), *Proceedings of the 2002 ICAME Conference*, Gothenburg.

Leech, G. and Fallon, R. (1992) 'Computer corpora – What do they tell us about culture?' *ICAME journal* 16: 29–50.

Leech, G. and Garside, R. (1991) 'Running a grammar factory: the production of syntactically analyzed corpora or "treebanks"', in S. Johansson and A-B. Stenström (eds), *English computer corpora*, Berlin: Mouton de Gruyter.

Lezius, W. (2000) 'Morphy – German morphology, part-of-speech tagging and applications', in U. Heid, S. Evert, E. Lehmann and C. Rohrer (eds), *Proceedings of the 9th EURALEX international congress*, Stuttgart, Germany, pp. 619–23.

Louw, B. (1993) 'Irony in the text or insincerity in the writer? The diagnostic potential of semantic prosodies', in M. Baker et al. (eds), *Text and technology*, Amsterdam: Benjamins, pp. 157–76.

Louw, B. (1997) 'The role of corpora in critical literary appreciation', in A. Wichmann, S. Fligelstone, T. McEnery and G. Knowles (eds), *Teaching and language corpora*, London: Longman, pp. 140–251.

MacWhinney, B. (1991) *The CHILDES project: tools for analyzing talk*, Hillsdale, NJ: Lawrence Erlbaum Associates.

McArthur, T. (1981) *Longman lexicon of contemporary English*, London: Longman.

McEnery, T. and Wilson, A. (1996) *Corpus linguistics*, Edinburgh: Edinburgh University Press.

McEnery, A. M., Xiao, R. and Tono, Y. (2005) *Corpus-based language studies*, Routledge: London.

Milde, J-T. and Gut, U. B. (2002) 'A prosodic corpus of non-native speech', in B. Bel and I. Marlien (eds), *Proceedings of the speech prosody 2002 conference*, 11–13 April 2002, Aix-en-Provence: laboratoire Parole et Language, pp. 503–6.

Milić, L. T. (1990) 'The century of prose corpus', *Literary and linguistic computing* 5: 3, 203–8.

Milton, J. C. and Tong, K. S. T. (eds) (1991) *Text analysis in computer-assisted language learning: Applications, qualifications and developments,* Hong Kong: Language Centre, Hong Kong University of Science and Technology.

Mindt, D. (1996) 'English corpus linguistics and the foreign language teaching syllabus', in J. Thomas and M. Short (eds), *Using corpora for language research*, London: Longman, pp. 232–47.

Murison-Bowie, S. (1993) *Micro-concord manual: An introduction to the practices and principles of concordancing in language teaching*, Oxford: Oxford University Press.

Oakes, M. (1998) *Statistics for corpus linguistics*, Edinburgh: Edinburgh University Press.

Oostdijk, N. (1991) *Corpus linguistics and the automatic analysis of English*, Amsterdam: Rodopi.

Pienemann, M. (1992) 'COALA – A computational system for inter-language analysis', *Second language research* 8: 1, 9–92.

Preyer, W. (1889) *The mind of a child*, New York: Appleton.

Pustejovsky, J., Bergler, S. and Anick, P. (1993) 'Lexical semantic techniques for corpus analysis', in *Computational linguistics*, Special issue on using large corpora II, 19: 2, 331–58.

Quirk, R. (1960) 'Towards a description of English usage', *Transactions of the Philological Society* 58: 2, pp. 50–61.

Quirk, R., Greenbaum, S., Leech, G. and Svartvik, J. (1985) *A comprehensive grammar of the English language*, London: Longman.

Ratnaparkhi, A. (1996) 'A maximum entropy part-of-speech tagger', in *Proceedings of the empirical methods in natural language processing conference*, University of Pennsylvania, 17–18 May 1996.

Renouf, A. (1993) 'A word in time: First findings from the investigation of dynamic text', in J. Aarts, P. de Haan and N. Oostdijk (eds), *English language corpora: Design, analysis and exploitation*, Amsterdam: Rodopi.

Reppen, R. and Ide, N. (2004) 'The American national corpus: An overview and the first release', *Journal of English linguistics* 32: 105–13.

Rissanen, M. (1992) 'The diachronic corpus as a window to the history of English', in K. Aijmer and B. Altenberg (eds), *English corpus linguistics: Studies in honour of Jan Svartvik*, London: Longman, pp. 128–43.

Sampson, G. (1995) *English for the computer*, Oxford: Oxford University Press.

Schmied, Josef (1994) 'The Lampeter corpus of early modern English tracts', in M. Kytö, M. Rissanen and S. Wright (eds), *Corpora across the centuries. Proceedings of the first international colloquium on English diachronic corpora*, St Catharine's College, Cambridge (25–27 March 1993), Amsterdam and Atlanta: Rodopi, pp. 81–9.

Scott, M. (1999) *WordSmith tools help manual*, Version 3.0, Oxford: Mike Scott and Oxford University Press.

Seiber, J. E. (1992) *Planning ethically responsible research*. London: Sage.

Sekine, S. and Grisham, R. (1995) 'A corpus-based probabilistic grammar with only two non-terminals', *Fourth international workshop on parsing technology*, Prague: ACL/SIGPARSE.

Selinker, L. (1974) 'Interlanguage', in J. Richards (ed.), *Error analysis: Perspectives on second language acquisition,* Essex: Longman, pp. 31–54.

Shalom, C. (1997) 'That great supermarket of desire: attributes of the desired other in personal advertisements', in K. Harvey and C. Shalom (eds), *Language and desire*, London: Routledge, pp. 186–203.

Simard, M. G., Foster, G. I. and Isabelle, P. (1992) 'Using cognates to align sentences in bilingual corpora', in *Proceedings of TMI-92*.

Simov, K., Osenova, P., Simov, A., Ivanova, K., Grigorov, I. and Ganev, H. (2004a) 'Creation of a tagged corpus for less-processed languages with CLaRK System', in *Proceedings of SALTMIL workshop at LREC 2004: First steps in language documentation for minority languages*, Lisbon, Portugal, pp. 80–3.

Simov, K., Simov, A., Ganev, H., Ivanova K. and Grigorov, I. (2004b) 'The CLaRK System: XML-based Corpora Development System for Rapid Prototyping', in *Proceedings of LREC04*, Lisbon, Portugal.

Sinclair, J. McH. (1991) *Corpus, concordance, collocation*, Oxford: Oxford University Press.

Sinclair, J. McH. (1996) 'The search for units of meaning', *Textus 9*: 75–106.

Sinclair, J. McH. (1999) 'A way with common words', in H. Hasselgård and S. Oksefjell (eds), *Out of corpora: Studies in honour of Stig Johnasson*, Amsterdam: Rodopi, pp. 157–79.

Sinclair, J. McH. and Renouf, A. (1988) 'A lexical syllabus for language learning', in R. Carter and M. McCarthy (eds), *Vocabulary and language teaching*, London: Longman, pp. 140–58.

Sleator, D. and Temperley, D. (1991) *Parsing English with a link grammar. Carnegie Mellon university computer science technical report*, CMU-CS-91-196, October 1991.

Smith, N. (1997) 'Improving a tagger', in R. Garside, G. Leech and A. McEnery (eds), *Corpus annotation: Linguistic information from computer text corpora*, London: Longman, pp. 137–50.

Smith, N., McEnery, T. and Ivanic, R. (1968) Issues in transcribing a corpus of children's handwritten projects, *Literary and linguistic computing* 13: 4, 217–26.

Sperberg-McQueen, C. M. and Burnard, L. (eds) (2002) *TEI P4: Guidelines for electronic text encoding and interchange*, Oxford,

Providence, Charlottesville, Bergen: Text Encoding Initiative Consortium. XML Version.

Stenström, A-B. (1984) 'Discourse items and pauses', paper presented at Fifth ICAME Conference, Windermere. Abstract in *ICAME News* 9 (1985): 11.

Stenström, A-B. (1987) 'Carry-on signals in English conversation', in W. Meijs (ed.), *Corpus linguistics and beyond*, Amsterdam: Rodopi, pp. 87–119.

Stern, W. (1924) *Psychology of early childhood up to six years of age*, New York: Holt.

Stubbs, M. (1996) *Text and corpus analysis*, London: Blackwell.

Stubbs, M. (2001) *Words and phrases*, London, Blackwell.

Svartvik, J. 1990a (ed.) *The London–Lund corpus of spoken English: Description and research. Lund studies in English 82*, Lund: Lund University.

Svartvik, J. 1990b 'Tagging and parsing on the TESS project', in J. Svartvik (ed.), *The London–Lund corpus of spoken English: Description and research. Lund studies in English 82*, Lund: Lund University, pp. 87–106.

Thorndike, E. L. and Lorge, I. (1944) *A Teacher's Word Book of 30,000 words*, New York: Columbia Teachers College.

Tognini-Bonelli, E. (2001). *Corpus linguistics at work (Studies in Corpus Linguistics: 6)*, Amsterdam/Atlanta, GA: John Benjamins.

Tribble, C. and Jones, G. (1990) *Concordances in the classroom. A guide to varieties of standard English*, London: Edward Arnold.

Ure, J. (1971) 'Lexical density and register differentiation', in G. Perren and J. L. M. Trim (eds), *Applications of linguistics*, London: Cambridge University Press, pp. 443–52.

van Halteren, H. (1999) 'Performance of taggers', in H. van Halteren (ed.), *Syntactic wordclass tagging*, Dordrecht: Kluwer Academic Publishers, pp. 81–94.

van Halteren, H. and van den Heuvel, T. (1990) *Linguistic exploitation of syntactic databases: The use of the Nijmegen linguistic database program*, Amsterdam: Rodopi.

van Rijsbergen, C. J. (1979) *Information retrieval*, Butterworth: London.

Voutilainen, A. (1993) 'NPtool. A detector of English noun phrases', in *Proceedings of the workshop on very large corpora*, Columbus, OH: Ohio State University, 22 June 1993, pp. 42–51.

Willett, P. (1988) 'Recent trends in hierarchic document clustering: A critical review', *Information Processing and Management* 24: 5, 577–97.

Willis, J. and Willis, D. (1996) *Challenge and change in language teach-*

ing, London: Heinemann.

Wilson, A. and Rayson, P. (1993) 'Automatic content analysis of spoken discourse: A report on work in progress', in C. Souter and E. Atwell (eds), *Corpus based computational linguistics*, Amsterdam: Rodopi, pp. 215–26.

Wilson, A. and Thomas, J. (1997) 'Semantic annotation', in R. Garside, G. Leech and A. McEnery (eds), *Corpus annotation: Linguistic information from computer texts*, London: Longman, pp. 55–65.

Woolls, D. (2000) 'From purity to pragmatism: user-driven development of a multilingual parallel concordancer', in S. Botley, A. M. McEnery and A. Wilson (eds), *Multilingual corpora in teaching and research*, Amsterdam: Rodopi, pp. 116–33.

Woolls, D. and Coulthard, M. (1998) 'Tools for the trade', *Forensic linguistics* 5: 33–57.